Blue as the Lake

Robert B. Stepto

A PERSONAL GEOGRAPHY

Blue

as the Lake

BEACON PRESS
BOSTON

Beacon Press
25 Beacon Street
Boston, Massachusetts 02108-2892
www.beacon.org

Beacon Press books
are published under the auspices of
the Unitarian Universalist Association of Congregations.

03 02 01 00 99   8 7 6 5 4 3 2

This book is printed on recycled acid-free paper that contains at least
20 percent postconsumer waste and meets the uncoated paper
ANSI/NISO specifications for permanence as revised in 1992.

Text design by Lucinda Hitchcock
Composition by Wilsted & Taylor Publishing Services

LIBRARY OF CONGRESS CATALOGING-IN-PUBLICATION DATA
Stepto, Robert B.
    Blue as the lake : a personal geography/Robert B. Stepto.
        p. cm.
    ISBN 0-8070-0944-X
    ISBN 0-8070-0945-8 (paper)
    1. Stepto, Robert B.—Childhood and youth.   2. Afro-Americans—Biography.
3. Afro-Americans—Social life and customs.   4. Idlewild (Mich.)—Biography.
5. Chicago (Ill.)—Biography.   6. Baltimore (Md.)—Biography.   I. Title.
E185.97.S818A3   1998
973'.0496073'0092—dc21
    [B]   98–5870

For Michele

Contents

OPPOSITE: *Author with bicycle,
early days in Woodlawn, 1951*

I

Paths of One's Invention

Idlewild

It is summer again, and time to dream again of summers past. Lately, my mind keeps wandering back to the many boyhood summers I spent in Idlewild, Michigan, on the edge of the Manistee National Forest. Idlewild was in some ways a typical retreat. There was a lake of some size, a small commercial patch, and a few amusements—a roller rink, a supper club, a place to go horseback riding. But in one respect, Idlewild was and remains decidedly untypical. It is an all-black town of roughly three hundred people that swells to three thousand or more residents in the summer months—or so it did in the 1940s and 1950s. Most of us arrived at our families' cottages from Detroit and Chicago. But I remember summer friends from other cities such as Cleveland and Cincinnati, and you could always spy license plates informing you that there were black folks in town from just about anywhere within a two-day drive.

At this point in my life, Idlewild is but a dot on a good map, a dot beside the slightly larger dot of Baldwin, Michigan, which may be on the map only because it is the county seat of Lake County. My parents sold their lakefront house, incredibly a shade of pink with white shutters, matching my mother's pink and white DeSoto, in 1959 or 1960. My grandparents held on to their place—"Deerpath" (lots of cottages had names)—a little longer, no doubt because they had had it longer (since 1941), had transformed it from a flimsy structure to a sturdy home, and had dreams of retiring there. But when certain realities set in—the harshness of the winters, worse than Chicago; the need for older people to be near medical care *and* their children—"Deerpath" went up on the block as well. In my immediate family, reasons for selling were abundant: you kids don't want to go to the country anymore ("Well, yes, I did hate leaving my baseball team right in the thick of the season"); with the money, we can install central air-conditioning in the Chicago house ("OK"); endlessly entertaining family and friends is *no* vacation ("I guess it wasn't, but I didn't know that then . . ."). My grandparents, on the other hand, didn't talk about this change in their lives at all; selling "Deerpath," like selling soon thereafter the Chicago house they'd owned since the 1920s, was after all a wrenching concession to the mounting pressures of age. They didn't speak of that much, least of all to me, and it was only my grandmother who said things which led me later to think how devastating it was for them to face squarely that neither her dream of returning to Atlanta (she was Spelman College, class of 1906) nor her husband's dream of retiring to Idlewild was going to happen. They were stuck in Chicago, without central air-conditioning, at least until they moved into my parents' house, in the spring of 1966. It jolts me to recall that they both were eighty years old at the time.

But let me return to Idlewild, as I did the other day when my finger followed the line of Route 37 on a map, north from Grand Rapids, past Newaygo, past White Cloud (onion fields and a golf course), into Baldwin, with the lumberyard and dry goods store on the left of Main Street, the movie theater, bank, and ice cream parlor on the right, the courthouse and jail straight ahead. To get to Idlewild, you turn right, roughly a block before the courthouse, drive past the fish hatcheries, and then slow down terrifically for the sharp right turn around the huge oak. After the rodeo grounds, you can ease into a forty-mile-an-hour spin, the road isn't challenging, and that's good, because if you are interested, there is much of a subtle nature increasingly on view. If you want to know something about how black people live, year round, in northern Michigan, well, look to the left and right. Idlewild of the Lake and the summer and of the summer folk is still a few miles ahead.

I sometimes review my thoughts about how Idlewild came to be in the first place. There is a story, somewhat self-disparaging in a way black stories about blacks can be, contending that Idlewild was founded by runaway slaves who, after traveling north for agonizing weeks on end, were convinced that they had reached Canada. And so they settled, and dug out a life, prosperity being out of the question for them and whites, too, until, ironically, blacks with *some* money started to summer there, and needed the goods and services which the "natives" could supply. It wasn't Canada, but it wasn't America either: Idlewild had a black postmaster and an all-black fire department; Baldwin was lily white but, surprisingly for the 1950s, free of prejudice and racial tension. Perhaps I am forgetting something, or perhaps, as a youth, I was shielded from situations and confrontations. But I do not recall any lectures about how to behave in Baldwin (lectures of the sort drilled into me when I was about to go into certain parts of Chicago or its suburbs), and I do not recall any incidents in the stores, the movie theater, etc. One could say that the small businessmen of the area were simply too pragmatic to discourage the fat summer trade, albeit brought to them by blackfolk flush with coin from the Great Lakes cities. As a child, however, my simple view was that prejudice was a matter of geography, and that we were too far north for trouble.

But of course prejudice had played a role of a kind in the creation of Idlewild and black summer resorts like it. While blacks of some means did plan and take summer vacations, there was always the question of where to go, or where you could go, and the quality of the welcome once there. Simple matters—where to stay? where to eat?—never were really that simple, unless you stopped with relatives, as people still do. I remember an occasion in the 1950s when the whole family had to sleep in the car because the motels we had tried all were mysteriously full. The next morning, the insult continued when the first place we entered for breakfast wouldn't serve us. These things happened not in the Deep South, but in supposedly less treacherous places, Ohio and Pennsylvania. In the 1960s, when we were making the last of our family motor trips, I vividly recall how my father would stop at a gas station, just before we arrived at our destination, just so he could "clean up," and maybe put on a fresh shirt *and* a tie. The idea was that such "precautions" would minimize "incidents" at the hotel's check-in counter. And yes, it was a hotel, always a hotel; motels were too iffy, too problematic, probably because they were too often owner-operated.

If these were the perils of summer travel at mid-century,

we should not marvel at all at how serious and determined early-century blacks were about founding their own summer enclaves, notably Oak Bluffs on Martha's Vineyard and in the Midwest, Idlewild. Above and beyond the pleasures of fresh air and clear skies, of water sports and sylvan walks, these places offered the prospect of safe harbor for one's family, removed from the heat and dangers of urban life, and protected as well from random acts of racism in other vacation settings. But gratification for the "patriarchs" was not limited to what came from providing summers to family or owning additional property: some genuinely relaxed, had fun, and in many ways restored themselves. Charles W. Chesnutt, for example, the black novelist and lawyer from Cleveland, summered in Idlewild in the 1920s, and evidently found there much release from the affairs of business. His daughter, Helen, remembers her father's pleasurable unwinding this way: "At Idlewild Chesnutt relaxed in the clear, pine-scented, health-giving air. He spent his days fishing, sitting in an old willow chair at the end of his little pier, absorbing the golden sunshine and catching a bluegill now and then with a bamboo fishing pole. Or, feeling more energetic, he would row out into the lake in his flat-bottomed boat (Susan [his wife] had insisted on this type of boat) to cast for bass with rod and reel.... If the weather was rainy or too cold for fishing, he would sit before the log fire in the living room and read, or play solitaire, or do crossword puzzles, which he enjoyed immensely, calling in all the members of the family for assistance which he never needed at all."

Chesnutt's schedule of simple diversions was, my memory tells me, less sought and less available by the 1950s. But what Chesnutt desired and apparently got from summer life in the

Idlewild of the mid-1920s, was largely what my grandparents and their generation of summer folk were seeking when they bought or erected their cottages in the thirties and early forties. My grandfather, for example, never to my knowledge fished, but he and my grandmother did go deer watching at dawn and both loved board games at dusk; and the constant cottage improvement projects that occupied the hours in between gave my grandfather, a man otherwise cooped up in either a laboratory or a post office in Chicago, immense pleasure. My grandparents, like the Chesnutts, went to Idlewild not for bouts of parties and nightclubbing, but for the pleasures of rustic life. But by the late fifties, the resorters far outnumbered the rustics—or so it seemed. And I distinctly remember concluding, youth though I was, that everything I had heard about the perils of having your city neighborhood "change" apparently could apply as well to the village of your country cottage.

In another passage from her book about her father, one that startled me upon first reading since my memories of Idlewild are of another, later time, Helen Chesnutt writes: "Nature was lavish at Idlewild. Brilliant blue skies reflected in the lake; the most gorgeous sunsets imaginable, fading away gradually to let the night come on, its sky studded thickly with brilliant stars and constellations that a city-dweller could never dream of. The sunrise was equally beautiful if one rose early enough. Nothing could surpass the thrill of seeing at that hour a crane stepping daintily along the shore of the lake, stopping now and then to dip its bill into the water in search of breakfast." Some of this rings true for me. What I know—and everything I have forgotten—about the stars and their constellations I learned in Idlewild at night, at the end of a pier or in the middle of a field or just outside the door of a cottage. The books that guided my seeing were from Chicago, but what I saw and printed on my brain I saw as a youth in the Idlewild of my summers. The touch about the breakfasting crane, however, stretches my credulity, though I guess such sights were possible before my time at the lake. The birds I saw which I never glimpsed in the city were usually woodland birds, high in the branches of some oak or birch, or ducks flying in formation across the sky, just above the pines on the point across the lake. In other words, the birds I recall were never quite as extraordinary as Helen Chesnutt's crane, and I don't recall that they were ever quite as at home on the lake as was her crane. However, what is most befuddling for me about Ms. Chesnutt's description is that it is so unqualified in its praise, so untainted by the onslaught of counter-memories of, say, a couple of beer cans, bobbing in the lake in uncanny rhythm with the dipping motions of the crane. This is not to say that Chesnutt's memories are suspect, for I can imagine a time when Idlewild was pristine. But in my day, I would have seen the beer cans and *maybe* the crane, and that in itself places me in another time, another Idlewild.

By the 1950s, Idlewild was noisy. The part known as the island, which had been a focal point since the 1920s primarily because the Clubhouse (a place for business meetings among lot owners, but also a place for dances and boardinghouse-style meals, especially in the early years) was there, was by then a strip of bars, nightclubs, and cafés, anchored on one end by a hotel and on the other by a roller rink, which I believe was occupying the original Clubhouse building. If the genteel Charles Chesnutt had still been alive. I'm sure he would have been apoplectic about the blaring rock and roll music from the roller rink, which didn't so much drift as charge across the lake, invading cottages a mile away. I think, too, given the religiously sedate man that he was, Chesnutt would have been astonished to hear daily through the trees and across the waters the evening broadcast of "Ave Maria," emanating from the PA system in the belfry of the evangelical church near the post office.

But there was more, for in addition to the cacophony of "Ave Maria" competing with the roller rink's "Why Do Fools Fall in Love"—truly an instance of dueling sound systems, as both sides must have admitted in secret—there was the nerve-rattling scream of the huge horn atop the volunteer fire department everyday at six, not counting, of course, the times it went off when there was actually a fire. Beyond that, there was the constant din, from the island specifically, of honky-tonk-cabaret street life. While we might have been in the country, there was clearly as much gaiety—loud, raucous, and sometimes dangerous gaiety—as there was along any strip of bars and clubs in urban Negro America. Indeed, there is a certain irony about me and other youths being protected from all of that "adult behavior" in Chicago, Detroit *et al.*, only to be exposed to it while on "fresh air holiday" in the woods. Later in life, when I found myself taking everything in at night on, say, Chicago's 47th Street or Harlem's 125th, I could say to myself, "This reminds me of the country, of being in Idlewild."

Another form of what we would now call noise pollution (and environmental pollution, too) was the motorboat. I report this with mixed emotions, for I then loved motorboats, and constantly designed and redesigned all sorts of power-craft in the leaves of the sketchbooks received as presents, especially after I forsook piano lessons on the South Side for drawing (and painting and sculpture) lessons downtown in Chicago's Loop. So ardent was my interest, fueled by afternoons along the shores of Lake Idlewild, and Lake Michigan, too, that occasionally I would take the money that would have purchased several comic books and buy a copy of *Motorboating* instead. These purchases invariably occurred on Saturdays, after art school, in the Van Buren Street Station of the Illinois Central Electric (the "IC"), while I was on my way home. *Motorboating*, along with a few captivating issues of *Yachting*, provided a cornucopia of aquamarine fantasies, whether by critiquing a particular boat, analyzing some new lethal Chrysler inboard engine, or describing an incredible race or excursion —on ocean or fresh waters, I didn't care.

It must have been out of some number of *Motorboating* that I got an accurate address for the Chris-Craft Corporation, for soon thereafter, with what can only be called a youth's innocence and impetuosity, I sent to Chris-Craft several of my designs. As I remember them, they were for rakish powercraft of the thirty-to-forty-foot class. What distinguished them from what Chris-Craft and their competitors were producing was more power (of course), and wrap-around windscreens, identical to the wrap-around windshields that were then appearing on Detroit automobiles, including my father's new Oldsmobile. Much to my pleasure and astonishment, I received a reply from Chris-Craft. It said in effect—and I wish to hell I knew where I put that letter—that the designs were promising and that I should contact Chris-Craft when I finished college. (Apparently, I must have put in my letter something like, "I hope you like my boats—I am only ten years old.") A decade later, in the last months of college, I found myself choosing among seminary, law school, and graduate study in English—naval architecture was no longer a part of my dreams or options. But I thank the man at Chris-Craft for taking five minutes to write a kind note to a dreaming boy; it was a decent thing to do.

Given all this, you can imagine my rapture when an uncle, the only family member to serve in the Navy, arrived one summer with a handsome Thompson clinker in tow behind his Studebaker. Rolling back the tarp for the first time was like opening a huge Christmas present, for stowed inside, cradled by the ribs of gleaming wood, were all sorts of marine paraphernalia—cushions, lifejackets, a gas tank, and yes, a Johnson outboard motor of reasonable power. With the arrival of Uncle Rog and the Thompson, my days *on* the lake began, as did my education about boat safety, boat maintenance, about how to read the water for shallows and submerged objects (I nevertheless sheared at least two propeller pins), and about how "half of the Negroes on this lake don't know squat about how to care for the boats they keep buying." With all the lessons and all the cautions, I was like a pup on a leash. But it didn't matter, for as far as *this* pup was concerned, it was more important to be out of the kennel and on a walk.

Sometimes we didn't dare go out on the lake: it was too treacherous—not because of the weather, but because of the near gridlock of boats whizzing the waters. There were a lot of daredevil maneuvers (some people freely do things in a boat they'd never do in a car), often bringing fast boats perilously close to swimmers, piers, and to each other. And there was a lot of slow-speed styling: people who knew how to drive a turquoise Cadillac at twenty miles an hour down an urban avenue also knew a lot about how to purr a Chris-Craft inboard along the edges of the lake, at just the speed that would allow onlookers to check out the driver's resort clothes and process, and to agree that the fine sister on the back cushion was indeed last month's centerfold in *Jet* magazine. Memories such as these make it hard for me to imagine Charles Chesnutt out on the lake in his flat-bottom rowboat—rowboaters often were nearly swamped by the buffeting wakes of the fast boats—or sitting at the end of his pier in a willow chair, trying to catch bluegill. That might have been possible in the twenties, but by the fifties, during the season at least, a pier was not a site for fishing but rather a seat for the show—the parade of bloods in boats, doing anything and everything as long as they didn't get their hair wet.

Accounts of Idlewild's early years mention mostly either the elderly cottagers, pursuing their version of life on Golden Pond, or the entrepreneurs who built the nightclubs which in time made Idlewild a desired booking for many black entertainers who appeared in big-city clubs and theaters, including Chicago's Regal and Harlem's Apollo. The accounts also remind us of the distinguished Negroes who were variously involved in Idlewild's development and destiny. Dr. Daniel Hale Williams, for example, the noted pioneer heart surgeon from Chicago, owned a magnificent home on the lake called Oakmere, and bought many lots which he eventually sold for a tidy profit. Dr. W. E. B. Du Bois, the extraordinary historian, sociologist, political economist, and editor of the NAACP's *Crisis* magazine, bought Idlewild lots for investment purposes, and even put in writing his praise of the white capitalists (Erastus Branch, Adelbert Branch, Wilbert Lemon, Mamye Lemon, Alvin Wright, and Madolin Wright) who had formed the Idlewild Resort Company in 1912 in order to purchase the black resort's original 2,700 acres, plus the lake. Du Bois was no great friend of American capitalism, but perhaps his endorsement of the Idlewild Resort Company can be explained by noting that the company sold the resort, rather soon as these things go, in 1921 to the all-black Idlewild Lot Owners Association, to which Du Bois belonged as long as he owned his lots. Celebrities, including athletes and stars of the stage and music world, made investments as well, though to my knowledge, they rarely built summer or retirement homes on their land, even when they owned coveted lakefront properties. This often vexed the people owning adjoining land who had cottages, and who naturally were anxious about whether another cottage suddenly was going to go up, sometimes just a stone's throw away. My parents, for example, after buying a house of their own in Idlewild, near my grandparents and on the lake, tried repeatedly to protect their privacy by purchasing the lot just north of them, owned by Lil Armstrong, Louis Armstrong's former wife. She refused their offers, and they had to settle into the hope that she would neither sell to someone else nor crowd a cottage in between us and the elderly woman presently next door.

Perhaps there were some truly distinguished summer residents in the Idlewild of my days, but I wasn't aware of them. Daniel Hale Williams and Charles Chesnutt were of course long gone, but what surprises me is that people that famous left so few traces of themselves. I do not remember, for example, overhearing adults saying things like, "That used to be Dr. Williams's place," or "Did you know Miss So-and-So is one of Chesnutt's granddaughters?" When I ask my parents where Dr. Williams's Oakmere was located, thinking they might know because of the Chicago connection and because of my father's affiliation with the hospital Williams helped to found, they say, "I don't know." When I push the matter and ask, "Well, can you at least tell me which side of the lake he was on?" my mother says, "Our side, I think," while my father replies, "That was before my time." Of course, there is somebody out there who can tell me, and there are property records, too, but that is not the point: the point is that Idlewild's elite pioneers had a way of not just dying but vanishing. And yet, consider this as well: the 1950s were not a time when black Americans put much effort into preserving or recovering their history, and probably doubted that the history of a black resort was history at all. Perhaps, too, the *carpe diem* mentality of being on vacation or seeking retirement stifled any sort of communal historical awareness. At any rate, in my youthful days on the lake, the collective focus was on the present and there were no ghosts from the past. Moreover, for me at least, the people who stood out were neither the respectable black professionals from the cities nor the flamboyant entertainers from what used to be called the "chittlin' circuit." I was fascinated instead by the handful of mystery men, the black Jay Gatsbys who sprang, as Fitzgerald's character did, from Platonic conceptions of themselves, apparently to serve as Gatsby did obsessively, "a vast, vulgar, and meretricious beauty." One such Gatsby lived just two piers away from us, and it was all I could do not to stop and stare when he appeared.

Milton Winfield—Mister Winfield—was a quiet, private man who nonetheless had subtle ways of calling attention to himself. There were plenty of Cadillacs in Idlewild, but Mr. Winfield's was one of the few of a somber color, and one of the few that seemed to be simply about its owner's need for proper transportation. Of course, the fact that Mr. Winfield sometimes had a driver at the wheel, a man built like a prizefighter who probably was a bodyguard, put him and his motorcar in a class of their own.

Mr. Winfield also had an imposing house, a real house in comparison to the summer cottages. There could be no doubt that it was weatherized, furnaced, and provisioned for sojourns in the country in any season, including trips of an urgent spontaneous sort. The house was white with blue trim; there were plantings and a lawn (I cannot remember another lawn in town, groomed and well cared for). It may have possessed a second story—unheard of in a resort village where some folks still didn't have indoor plumbing. While I'm not sure of the second story, with its suggestion of airy bedrooms with lake views, I am certain about the fence surrounding the property. Fences weren't entirely unusual; my grandfather, for example, had put up a wooden rail fence which did nothing more than please the eye and define a few boundaries. It was a horse country fence. In contrast, Mr. Winfield's was a formidable chainlink fence, as high as what you see around a tennis court, only the fence was not for confining sports activities to the grounds, but clearly for keeping people out. I doubt that the fence was supplemented by an intruder alarm system, but if any resident of Idlewild had such a system in the 1950s, Milton Winfield did.

Given the armatures and public style of the man, I was always pleased when Mr. Winfield gave me a little nod or wave. I felt I had a little arrangement, a small piece of business going, with the local padrone. But my place in his world was always clear, for the nods and waves never led to conversations, let alone to avuncular kindnesses such as outings in his sleek boat. I was surprised to learn much later on, from my father, that Mr. Winfield had a son, for I had never seen a son, and I don't even remember a Mrs. Winfield—a wife. I had always assumed that Mr. Winfield had no family, and didn't want any. That, too, was what the chain link fence was about.

The first time the police came was early on a sunny morning. I was up and dressed because it was fun to trot over to my grandparents' cottage, before my mother rose, for a biscuit or a plate of fried apples. They came in three or four cars, stealthily yet swiftly, decelerating from forty miles an hour to zero and stopping, at strategic points around the perimeter of Mr. Winfield's property, with the quiet of cats finding themselves just yards away from prey. One or two cops ran through our neighbor's lot—or maybe it was *our* lot—to cover the rear, which was Mr. Winfield's door and cascading steps to the lake. The rest marched to the front door, and, for all I know, rang the bell.

I anticipated a shoot-out. I thought that if I could hide behind a pine tree, or behind my mother's DeSoto, I could watch while a dozen erstwhile black prizefighters thrust rifles or machine guns out of Mr. Winfield's windows and fired on a bunch of white Chicago cops while they took cover behind their big Fords and drew their weapons. It would be a whole lot to check out before going horseback riding at ten, and a monstrous story to tell once back on the block in Chicago.

But nothing happened—Mr. Winfield wasn't there, and the cops packed up and left. When they came again, and again, he wasn't there either. But I am certain that at least one time, maybe more, after the cops departed, Mr. Winfield soon thereafter came down the steps to the lake with one of his burly men. After unlocking the gate in the fence, he went out on his concrete pier, where his inboard launch lay, wrapped up and hulking. After firing up the boat and donning a yachts-man's cap, he assumed the wheel and took what might be called a victory lap around the lake.

Perhaps it is odd to associate boyhood summers with reading and learning, but this is much the case for me. Every morning, after the chores, I was free to head out for wherever on my bicycle, the sole condition being that I return home at a designated hour for a proper lunch and an hour's worth of reading in my bunk. After the reading hour, I could again jump upon my bicycle and adventure around until the firehouse whistle blew at six. Then it was my solemn duty to tear myself away from whatever board game, ball game, or nightclub rehearsal was enthralling me, and to pedal home briskly. Later in the evening, perhaps after a twilight spin in the boat, or after giving up on finding something good on the radio, I would return to my book, more curious about the next chapter than I ever wanted all the schoolteachers in the family to know. My mother would come into my room and exclaim with unconcealed delight, "Oh, you're reading." I wanted to growl back, "Yeah, well, don't get the wrong impression—I'm just passing the time."

The whole summer reading project—the parent's insistence, the child's complaints and footdragging, and then the child's seduction—began in June in Chicago, during the days after school ended, when preparations for going to Idlewild began in earnest. The Chicago public library system had in those days a summer book loan plan which allowed kids (and maybe adults, too) to check out twenty or thirty books for the entire summer. My mother, a public school reading teacher, considered this to be the best uplift scheme since Tuskegee, and so there was no question as to whether I would appear on one of the check-out days at the Kimbark branch library with my library card, and a duffel bag to be filled to the zipper.

One such trip stands out in my mind because it was a sunny, hot day, and I had to walk both legs of the trip. Walking to the library probably was a delight. I imagine I veritably skipped along, taking in all I liked to observe along the route: the Wedgewood Towers Hotel (a kind of flatiron building wedged in the V created at 64th Street where Minerva Avenue veered off Woodlawn), where Minnie Minoso and a few other black baseball players lived—sometimes you could see them up close or admire Minoso's pink Cadillac; the music store on 63rd Street, which still had a ceramic RCA Victor dog outside its entrance; the marquee of the Kimbark Theater (cartoons and cowboy movies had not yet given way to the all-Spanish programs run in our last years in the neighborhood). However, the walk *back* was another matter: the duffel bag brimmed with books (given the kind of kid I was, it never occurred to me that I could undo this whole project by returning with only a book or two) and I was truly struggling with the bulk and weight. The heat didn't help, and matters became worse when a handle broke off the bag.

And so I was toiling home, carrying a huge bag of books in my arms in the manner of a child struggling with heavy groceries or firewood, or with an infant brother or sister, burdens we all remember because when the hefting becomes *work*, we say things like: "I don't eat any of this stuff," or "Who needs a fire anyway?" or "I never wanted a kid brother/sister." Right at the point the books were becoming a true chore, some kids I vaguely knew from the library caught up with me. One or two of them had books in hand, but none was as stupid as me to be laboring along with a whole satchel full. While I toted my bale, they pranced like long-legged puppies, circling like pups do when they want a walker or a postman to drop everything and play.

One such pup I remember to be a saucy girl; she perused me several times while I was struggling, sweating, then said: "Hey, you sure have hairy arms." That set off a titter in the group, mortifying me. If the temperature had been ninety degrees moments before, it was now ninety-five. My arms were not especially hairy, and now I know, after having been out in the world a bit, my arms aren't especially hairy at all. But being at the time ten years old or so, and black, and of a black community, I was terribly sensitive not just about the hair on my arms but about the fact that the summer sun always quickly bleached them a dusty blond. That was some unexplainable, inexplicable stuff; and what could I do right then and there, my arms were exposed for all to see, since they enfolded the treasure of library books, burdening me then as they promised to do later once I was up north in the woods.

But the saucy girl wasn't through. She circled again, and let loose with, "Hey, with hairy arms like those, I'd sure like to see your *balls.*" Even now, I still cringe at the memory of how the banterers guffawed, how the books in my arms tripled in weight, of how I said next to nothing while melting like butter on the hot sidewalk. Just a few years later, when, say, thirteen or fourteen, I think I could have managed, even with the books in tow, an appropriate, even withering retort—a reply comparably sexual. But I wasn't ready then, and I was the one withered. We all indulge in the fantasy exercise of "what I should have said"; to this day, I fashion replies to that girl, wondering still what her name was.

Idlewild

Then there was Eddie Gray. Eddie is now a Chicago lawyer, living in the same townhouse complex where my Uncle Herman lives; he's a buddy I don't mind seeing when I'm back home. In the fifties, however, Eddie was more acquaintance than friend, perhaps because we went to different schools. We were aware of each other because we were acolytes at St. Edmund's, and because the network of black middle-class youth clubs, with its interminable schedule of holiday parties and wholesome events, had us forever bumping into each other. Yes, I knew Eddie, but having him up to our house in Idlewild and sharing my room for a fortnight was not my idea. It was the sort of thing parents cook up, and, indeed, Alice Gray and my mother were close enough friends to think such a visit a "great idea."

So it came to pass that Alice and Eddie arrived one day in Idlewild, and I had to be couth enough to greet him cheerfully while showing him to what had suddenly become *our* room. As the days went by, I was less and less the good host. In fact, I was a raging ass. Eddie was not athletic, and so there was no chance that a game of catch with a baseball could turn into something splendid and rousing, complete with fly balls to be snared and ground balls to be deftly turned into double plays. Playing catch with Eddie was enormously about hoping that if you threw him the ball you might see it again, soon, and not after searching through the weeds with a stick. I got impatient, and started giving him a lot of crap whenever our mothers were out of earshot. For good measure, I started in on him about his weight—he was pudgy—and kept that up until one day tears welled in his eyes. Eventually, my mother grabbed me, took me outside, and gave me the talking-to I deserved. I agreed to behave—or to behave better—but I didn't change

· 21 ·

my mind about Eddie and the whole miserable visit: I wanted it to end, I wanted my room back, I was willing to suffer a whipping if that was the price I had to pay to hear the sound of Alice and Eddie packing to go.

But one afternoon, I did change my mind about Eddie, unexpectedly, during the reading hour. Eddie apparently was on the same uplift schedule I was, and had some books with him. I was curious about what he was reading, and was dumbstruck, after glancing at the pages of his book, to realize that he was reading poetry. I asked him who the poet was; he replied, "Paul Laurence Dunbar." I confessed I'd never heard of him. Eddie then told me what seemed like a great deal about Dunbar. What I remember best is that he spoke not like a young student into whom some facts have been poured, but absolutely like someone who knew Dunbar because he had *read* Dunbar, and had entered into some sort of company with him. What I recall, too, is that Eddie rose from his chair, and, while strolling the room, recited from memory Dunbar's "Little Brown Baby With the Sparklin' Eyes."

This is a memory that returns to me most every summer, and certainly every fall, for it is in the fall that I teach my Modern African American Poets course, and Dunbar is the first poet encountered. A year ago, a student I rather like came up to me after the Dunbar classes and said, "I enjoyed the Dunbar but must ask you why you didn't assign 'Little Brown Baby With the Sparklin' Eyes'? It's my favorite Dunbar poem." I replied, "It's one of my favorites, too." But of course I hadn't answered her question, and I knew that as soon as I thought about our conversation while walking back to my office. Why *don't* I teach that poem? Is it because it doesn't fit into what I want to say about Dunbar? Or is the reason less pedagogical, less professional?

The poem seems to be for me Eddie Gray's poem. And while I could doubtlessly say more about the poem today than he did when we were ten or eleven, I seem to be willing to leave it alone, so that what Eddie taught me about it and himself may remain intact.

Summer reading also brought me and a boy named Mike together. But maybe I should say that reading brought Mike to me, since he was always coming over to our cottage and poring over everything on the bookshelves and in the magazine racks. I liked Mike—he was a good fellow to know for bike rides, fishing, and for ways to sneak in afternoon nightclub rehearsals. But his nose-in-a-book routine, in full view of elders, was very annoying; I didn't need any behavior from friends that called into question my own commitments. Indeed, it was right about the time I felt I had succeeded in convincing everyone that no normal boy on summer vacation read more than an hour a day, that Mike started coming over to scan the shelves, hardly knowing what grand act of sabotage he was committing.

Like Eddie, Mike was from Chicago. But our buddyship was strictly one of summertimes up north in the woods. Once, in Chicago, we ran into each other in the lobby of a movie theater, and were stunned to discover that outside Idlewild we barely knew how to speak to each other—conversation was forced and virtually impossible. I recall once trying to bridge this gulf by inviting Mike over to my house one wintry Saturday—or maybe the invitation was for us to go to the movies together, perhaps (although I couldn't have put it this way then) to repair the awkward moments we'd had in a theater before. But Mike couldn't come — he wasn't allowed out that day. He seemed, in our few, brief telephone conversations in Chicago, more confined to his house and more shackled by chores than he ever was in Idlewild, if that was possible. His anxious, almost whispered, replies to my cheery hailings told me that.

Mike's circumstance was that both parents were dead, or might as well have been, and he was living with a grandmother who was clearly angry about having to raise him. I am certain she wanted the best for him, and saw that the best might come from a thorough grounding in regimen, routine, and responsibility. But anger was mixed in the schedule as well; there were too few kind words from her to think otherwise. Mike's grandmother was obviously a woman of property — houses both in Chicago and in Idlewild — and evidently had the income, albeit probably a retirement income, to maintain the houses, herself, and Mike. But money was always an issue, or was *made* an issue. I soon became careful in Idlewild about suggesting that we swing over to Ti-Jon's (the ice cream parlor) or to the general store for something cold on a hot day, for I knew that Mike probably had only 25 cents in his pocket and that that had to last him a week. Sometimes Mike bravely asked his grandmother for another quarter, and sometimes he got it. But having heard the sorts of interrogations he had to suffer for 25 cents, I decided that I would just as soon avoid playing a part in putting Mike in that position. Instead of going to the general store, we might as well repair back to my house. Perhaps this is how Mike first ended up at our cottage in the late afternoon, the seduction of a cold drink leading to his eager study of the books.

On one such afternoon, Mike picked up my copy of Bertha Morris Parker's *Golden Treasury of Natural History*. The book was hardbound and heavy, and while I often saw it to be one of my summer ball and chains, I had to admit that it had taught me all I knew about flora and fauna of the upper Midwest, and about birds and small animals, too. If I could walk as a youth along a country road in Idlewild, casually identifying every tree and most every bird, it was because Bertha Morris Parker's book was my trot, though I was damned if I was going to admit that in a manner approaching gratitude. After all, Ms. Parker was not just a renowned author but a science teacher at my school—the Laboratory School of the University of Chicago—and I was determined to keep my Chicago schoolteachers in place, bracketed outside of my Idlewild summers.

But Mike pored on through the Parker, and for my part, no proffered board game, no provocative conversation about, say, the young ladies in the neighborhood, could tear him away. I can see it all now, Mike bent over the book, his knees awkwardly crimped to keep it in place in his lap. Meanwhile, my relatives are glancing up from their bridge hands, to adore Mike and to frown at me, and then to nod approvingly to themselves, as if to say that despite Bobby's proclivities, they could play on with the bridge game, since thanks to Mike the race's fate was in good hands.

Around five, Mike had to leave. A gloom descended, for rather than accepting the explanation that Mike had to be home for dinner, we all believed that he had chores to perform with the chickens and other barnyard creatures. We fantasized furthermore that Mike might even have to patch a roof or pour a concrete walk before sundown. Perhaps it was this which charged somebody to step forward and say, "Mike, take the book with you. Bring it back in a few days, but take it with you."

Mike left, and an evening rain came. We had dinner and began to settle into what amused each on a rainy evening. I was noodling with the radio on the porch when, at twilight's last moment, Mike knocked at the door. I was surprised to see him, and he was mortified to be knocking. When I opened the screen door, he handed me back the Bertha Morris Parker book, now carefully wrapped to protect it against the steady rain. A relative burst out from the shadows and asked, "Why, Mike? I said you could borrow the book." "My grandmother says this is a fine book," he told us, when he finally spoke, "too fine to be in her house, too fine for me to read." With that, Mike walked away, having done what his grandmother wanted him to do, what he could do in response. My relatives stared at each other; I simply went to bed.

I don't think I read quite as much in the last year or two at Idlewild, though there were singular achievements such as working through all of Mark Twain and Sherlock Holmes. One distraction was the little portable television, now out on the porch: while my grandparents continued to ban all such modern appurtenances from their country life, my parents relented, and even installed a telephone as well. The TV picked up only one channel, the broadcast from Cadillac, Michigan, and that in itself monitored just how much television became a part of an evening's activity. However, the Cadillac station offered plenty of Detroit Tiger baseball games, and I must have watched at least three a week.

Then, too, there was "the girl next door"—actually, the

ravishing cousin of the girl next door. Sometimes in the evening, we would meet down by the lake and talk about everything and nothing while sitting on the end of the pier. After the sun went down, the few motorboats still on the lake would turn on their running lights and purr back to their docks, and we would sit a little closer. Of course, we could have done that while the boats were still on the lake, but we weren't going to risk that—we could be *seen,* and our "love" was supposed to be some Big Secret. Parents couldn't know about us, her boyfriend and my girlfriend (whoever they were) couldn't know, the entire cities of Chicago and Detroit (she was from there) had to be kept in the dark for sure, since after all we had to *return* to those places. On the other hand, the cousin—the real "girl next door"—*had* to know; because somebody had to know and be sworn to secrecy.

When it really was nighttime, we had to get cracking at whatever we were going to do to each other, since it would be only a matter of minutes before some parent would step out of a house, wondering where the children were. It was like petting with the kitchen timer going, only in this case the timer could not only beckon, but walk up and ask questions. But those were still sweet moments, moments filled with slow dancing on the beach to the tunes on the jukebox at the roller rink, moments that were all they could be—given the fact that the other girl from next door was there too, and, being twelve, we didn't know what to do about that.

My secret love of that summer turned out to be the first girl not from Chicago whose address I took and carefully memorized. I wrote her several times—long distance calls were never considered, as I have told my son when I see his phone bills to Barcelona—and she wrote back, on perfumed stationery no less. This kept up until maybe Thanksgiving, at which point we both decided, I guess, that the summer was over. But more than that was over, for it would be that winter that the Idlewild cottage would be sold. Thereafter, summer reading, writing, and dancing on the beach would occur in other territories, other climes.

When I talk with my mother about closing up the Idlewild house at summer's end, she says, "Oh yes, we used to go up and do that over Columbus Day weekend. There was no school on Monday." This puzzles me, mainly because since I attended private school, I never had Columbus Day off, as the public schoolers did. But maybe we did go up that weekend to put things in storage and to board up the windows: I certainly remember the change the fall brought to the air and to the lake, and perhaps those are October days I recall, not September ones. But September, too, was a time when the other summer people had gone, when the air had a nip in it, and we were in Idlewild. This was usually so because my school had not yet started (as part of the university it was on the university's quarter system schedule), and because, for a few years at least, my parents chose to stay up to the country through their anniversary, September 13th.

We never saw much of my father in August; I don't know what the statistics are for other parts of the country, but in August in Chicago, obstetricians are monstrously busy, delivering every baby created when the first winds of the last winter blew and folks naturally had to snuggle. He made up for this, sort of, by arriving during Labor Day weekend and staying on through the thirteenth. Having my father around was always a bit of an experiment, one which reminded me far too much of when I was four or five, and we moved out of my grandparents' house to a home of our own, the two-flat on Minerva Avenue. Suddenly, then, we were a nuclear family under one roof, not an extended family in the same house, and I didn't know what to think about it. Good thoughts were expected and possibly *de rigueur* (after all, we're talking about the fifties), but bad thoughts, negative assessments, were oh so tempting. I recall sitting in the midst of the construction of the new kitchen of the new home, sipping the worst glass of orange juice I had ever had (it was my first glass of frozen orange juice), and thinking, This isn't going to work. Where are Grandma and Grandpa?

Another version of this was soon played out in Idlewild. To be in Idlewild was to be back with my grandparents, to repair the rupture created when we moved out of their house and into our own. But when my parents bought their own home in Idlewild, three or four years after buying their own home in the city, I had to adjust once again to the concept, the bounding imperative, that a boy should live within the bordered place that gave his parents identity and ease. The realities of that were starkly evident in September, after summer playmates had left; after Uncle Rog departed with his boat; after Mr. Jones, who each year carted to Idlewild our various boxes and bicycles, came to retrieve the same; after Grandma and Grandpa were no longer just around the corner from the firehouse.

How did I pass the time, the interminable days of summer's end? I know I read, and in the last year or two at Idlewild watched baseball on the little television as the pennant races heated up. I felt lost without a bicycle, and doubted that a walk or a hike offered the same gratification as a fast spin along the blacktop road to the center of the village. But I learned how to take walks and how to find pleasure in them, even though I was sometimes astonished, stopped in my tracks even, to discover that I was walking and alone, and not biking with Mike and Eugene, cavorting and claiming the road as much as we dared, until a car honked us to the side.

Truly the most exciting thing I did in September was to ride in Sarge Johnson's horse round-up. Sarge was an Idlewild institution—a wizened old black man—a blind veteran of the Spanish-American War—who ran a stable from which you could go on horseback rides around the lake. You couldn't go anywhere else—or at least kids couldn't—and Mrs. Johnson, a brusque woman half Sarge's age, made sure you didn't by driving slowly along behind you in her Oldsmobile. Two honks from her and the horses commenced to trot; one honk later and they fell back into a walk, much to the relief of the tourist folk who didn't know how to post and usually got jostled up pretty bad. Some of them moaned, as people do in the midst of a rollercoaster ride; I was secretly amused by that, especially when the moaners were adults.

I rode the horses at Sarge's every summer of the 1950s, and reveled in advancing from the tottering, ancient mounts to the friskier horses requiring some skill to ride. In the last years, I had a "job" at Sarge's, leading strings of riders and horses on the route around the lake. My pay was that I rode for free, and I rode enough to have saddle sores, which I would vividly remember in the winter whenever a cowboy in a movie would creakingly climb out of a saddle. I knew what that was all about.

There were two of us boys who led horses around for Sarge, and when Mrs. Johnson found out that we would still be in Idlewild after Labor Day, we were asked to help with the round-up. Why it was called a round-up was even then something of a mystery, for we obviously didn't have to ride out into the sagebrush, as the movie cowboys did, to round up wild ponies for breaking or branding. And certainly there was no mythic black stallion holed up in some canyon that nobody had ever been able to put a rope on. Our task was to saddle up two horses and to herd the rest down ten miles or so of dirt roads I'd never been on, to a field simply known as The Pasture. In this, we were assisted, or rather overseen, by the ever-present Mrs. Johnson, who was never too far behind us in the Oldsmobile. What made this shadowing different, however, was that Sarge always came along with her for the round-up, as did their daughter, an adopted white girl of five or six, who was wild and boisterous, and whose presence in, say, Sarge's lap never failed to raise an eyebrow or two.

The boy riding with me was older, a teenager, and had ridden plenty of round-ups before I first came along, or so he convinced me. He took me aside and explained that late in the day, when we got closer to the pasture, the horses would realize that they weren't going for yet another trudge around the lake—they were going to horse heaven, The Pasture, the reward for putting up with a summer's worth of giddy kids and roaring adults, with daily saddlings and harnessings. At that point, he said, they would break into a canter, and some would run, and if we got far enough ahead of Mrs. Johnson, or around some big bend in the road, we could run our horses, too—just to catch up to the horses bolting ahead, of course—and that would be fun, more fun than I could imagine.

Things happened mostly that way. The round-up began with us squiring a dozen horses down familiar roads, and then around bends and up and down grades where I'd never been. At that point, we were just escorting the band, and I had plenty of opportunity to scan the landscape, taking in the scrub pine, white oak, birch, the wildflowers, the occasional rough house set back from the road; to wonder where I was and how far from Idlewild. But it was no time before the horses became frisky, agitated in fact. They would snort and prance; they would stroll up to some former stablemate and nip him or her, and maybe add a swift kick for good measure. With the kicking, the band became unruly, and I cautiously attempted to assume authority and impose order, as I had seen movie cowboys magically do with hundreds of cattle or scores of horses. But nothing worked. For one thing, I could see in the eyes of every horse that they thought I was a chump from the city who didn't know his ass from a stirrup and they weren't about to let me interfere with their pleasure. And for another thing, my horse, the liveliest horse I had graduated to riding, wasn't cooperating. I knew that when he suddenly veered in a direction quite opposite from that in which I thought I was reining him, and kicked the business out of a horse I couldn't imagine deserving such treatment. I just barely stayed in the saddle. My buddy, the teenager, just winked and chuckled, while riding and *controlling* Sarge's most majestic horse, riding handsomely, like John Wayne.

Soon thereafter, the dangerous cavorting stopped and the horses, sensing that they were near the pasture, raised their ears like antennae, and got serious about moving down the road. There were a few surprises: some horses that had been absolute dogs during the summer season, sullen about giving any rider the smallest thrill, took off almost like thoroughbreds. Other horses, the most sprightly and cantankerous, predictably were the first to run and indeed to stretch out in running; it was truly something to see them in their drive to leave summer and Idlewild behind. "Now's the time," my buddy said, and sprinted ahead like a jockey in a money race. I glanced behind to see how close Mrs. Johnson was in the car, and seeing that she wasn't close at all, slapped the reins, leaned into the mane of the roan I was riding, and just let things happen.

We were going fast; I was actually on a horse that was running full tilt. We weren't herding in the other running horses, we were passing them, breaking out for fresh territory. After maybe ten minutes of pure thrill and exhilaration, it occurred to me that I needed to rein in my horse. Otherwise, we weren't squiring the other horses to pasture, and I would catch hell from the Johnsons. But reining in was another thing that didn't work for me that day. When I pulled on the reins, and then really pulled, my horse began to buck and swerve. I was convinced it wanted to ditch me. And so I said, "All right, let's go," and leaned into the mane again, while the horse ran and ran and lathered.

I was riding at breathtaking speed, not knowing where in the world I was going. At one point, my buddy caught up and yelled, "Hey, cool it, the Johnsons are going crazy, you're running that horse too hard." Then the Oldsmobile pulled alongside of me, and Sarge leaned out. "Rein that horse in or I'm going to kick your ass." Profanity from adults always had great effect on me, but I feared more being thrown by an angry horse into a patch of poison ivy. That forced me to say to myself, "I'm riding this one out."

Then came a fork in the road. I didn't know which way to go, and my buddy and the Oldsmobile had drifted back behind me, perhaps to keep watch on the other horses. As the fork approached, I simply gave the horse its head; it knew where it was going, and went left. After a quarter mile, we swung into the pasture, and the lathered horse found enough energy to buck me off. I was still half-lying on the ground when the rest of the horses thundered in with the Oldsmobile right behind them.

The car ride back to Idlewild was excruciating. Sarge cursed me every minute of the way, and everyone else, including the buddy (now suddenly innocent of running *his* horse), had their own way of joining in. After I was dropped off at home, the Oldsmobile left with a roar and spewing of gravel. When I approached the kitchen door, tired and forlorn, my father asked, "What was *that* all about?"

Staying in Idlewild after Labor Day was dedicated to my parents' finally having some summertime together, and my walks and round-ups helped that happen. But there were family moments as well: trips to Ludington, and traipsings on the beaches and dunes there, and visits to the Dairy Queen for hot fudge sundaes. Then, too, there were the longer drives to Traverse City—about as far as we ever ventured from Idlewild—where there was a kind of North Country zoo, full of moose and elk and caribou. There was a sign on the fence boundarying the moose area that warned, "Don't Stand Close." One day I did, as curious kids will do, and got the scare of my life when a moose crashed into the fence, almost opening a hole in the chain link.

But what I remember best was the chilly September day my father and I went down the hill to our Idlewild beach and built a fire. I was delighted by the special lunacy of it: it was

cold and windy and the lake almost had whitecaps; everything pointed to retreating back to the house, building a fire
there, and maybe having a cup of cocoa. But we stayed down on
the beach and got a driftwood fire going and huddled around
it as if shelter was nowhere in sight. Then my father suggested
that we cook something. I scampered up the hill and found a
kielbasa in the refrigerator. Eventually, the makings for a
grand lunch were assembled, put in a sack, and carted out into
the chilly day and down to the beach. My father had cooked for
us, for me, only once before, during a harrowing time when
my mother was sick. This time was better; it was as good as it
would ever be.

Washington Park

After the first summers in Idlewild, I returned to Chicago to live with my parents, and also with Aunt Marge and Uncle Rog and my grandparents, in my grandparents' house: "Fifty-seven twenty-*two* Indiana Ave*nue*." The happy bounce of that jingle, so frequently rattled off by family members of any generation, reminds me of what a warm communal arrangement it was. The necessity of housing all seven of us produced the will to make it workable and genial; it was not a setting, in Robert Hayden's words, of "blueblack cold" and "chronic angers."

Grandma and Grandpa Burns lived in a neighborhood officially known as Washington Park, though I never heard anyone who resided there call it that. I myself first discovered that it was named Washington Park when, in a moment of true boredom around the age of ten, I started in reading the telephone book and discovered an "official" map of Chicago's neighborhoods. Finding out that I had lived, and that my grandparents continued to live, in a neighborhood with a *name* completely unknown to me bewildered and unmoored me. It was the first moment, the first sensing, of knowing that there could be mammoth discrepancies between the reality certain people lived and the reality of maps and other constructs. And the realities of the constructs were not to be dismissed: people *read* such abstractions, and accordingly make decisions, dole out largesse, and so forth. Down at City Hall, the Mayor (shall it be Kelly? Kennelly? even Daley?) growls, "Can we count on Washington Park?" and the functionaries from the neighborhood *better* be able to translate ("Washington Park," that's us!) and answer: "Yes, Mister Mayor, you can count on us; we'll vote early and often!"

While the people in the neighborhood had no particular name for it, I believe other people—other black people—did. The name or names were probably derogatory, for the neighborhood was, in the 1940s, "out south," meaning that it was south of the original, pre-1920, black ghetto. South by a mile or more of the corners of 47th Street and South Parkway (now Martin Luther King, Jr., Drive)—the crossroads of the district Gwendolyn Brooks and many others called Bronzeville; south enough even to be within the area serviced by an integrated high school, Englewood (my father was class of '38), though that (i.e., the racial composition) was soon to change. The playwright Lorraine Hansberry was a teenager in Washington Park around the time I was a toddler there, and in *To Be Young, Gifted, and Black* she describes an episode of frightening racial tension at Englewood. Matters became more volatile, and then quickly resolved, when cars full of black high schoolers arrived at Englewood from the Bronzeville high schools named for the black priest Jean Baptiste Point Du Sable and for the abolitionist Wendell Phillips. The Du Sable and Phillips students (". . . in their costumes of pegged pants and conked heads and tight skirts and almost knee-length sweaters and—worst of all—*colored* anklets, held up by rubber bands!") charged upon the scene because they were convinced, in Hansberry's words, that "THEM CHICKEN-SHIT NIGGERS OUT THERE AIN'T *ABOUT* TO FIGHT!" If that was what they truly thought, then heaven knows what else they called us— or what they called our neighborhood; surely not "Washington Park."

Of course, what they called us and thought of us had nothing to do with what we didn't have (and there were plenty of "have-nots" in Washington Park), and everything to do with what we had, or seemed to have. We were the black people who had been in Chicago for twenty or thirty years, or maybe had been born there (the case for my parents, for example), and were not necessarily being defeated by it. We were the Negroes "experimenting" with faiths other than Baptist and Methodist and otherwise supporting the churches in which the likes of Du Bois and James Weldon Johnson spoke when they came to town. We were the railroad workers and train porters, postal workers and social workers, small businessmen, schoolteachers, ministers, homemakers, and scant few doctors and lawyers insistent upon making of the neighborhood, if only for a moment's time, a ceremonial ground for uplift; we were hunkered down to "strive" for what parents and schools had taught was worth the effort.

According to a map in St. Clair Drake and Horace Cayton's study, *Black Metropolis*, while Washington Park was one of the several South Side neighborhoods into which Negroes were allowed to settle (encroach?) in the 1920s (my mother's family arrived there in 1928), it was virtually the only one in which black settlement, then, was greeted with violence. The reason for this, I believe, had less to do with the expansive, adjacent park, or with the still attractive apartment buildings, than with the presence of houses—single-family dwellings both attached and free-standing. Such houses were the repositories of American dreams—the most desirable sites for special acts of hearthing and nesting—for people of any race. Hence, the attacks, the bricks, the fires: white folks didn't want something as irrational as race to force them to move out; black folks didn't want something as predictable as race to keep them from moving in.

My grandparents' place on Indiana Avenue was indeed a house; a tidy, narrow, two-story brick affair with a limestone face to the street, with a wall in common with the house next door that was a mirror image of our house in terms of stairs, porch, windows, floor plan, and most everything else. Their place was indeed a house because, as my mother tells it, her mother insisted upon it: she was tired of living with her sister at 4545 Vincennes, a common enough arrangement for migrants to any big city—but an arrangement for how long? She was probably thinking, too, that if she was in Chicago to stay, and it was looking more and more that way, then she might as well begin to approximate in Chicago the house and household she had established in St. Joseph, Missouri, twenty years before. Of course, there wouldn't be the chickens, but maybe there could be much of what had been relinquished when Ocie, her husband, realized that even before the age of thirty he had exhausted his prospects in their hometown of St. Joe, despite or maybe *because* of his college degree.

So they moved to Chicago and later to Washington Park, timing matters, ordering their lives as family, church, Spelman, and Tuskegee had taught them to do. It was no mere co-incidence that they began to save and plan for a move right af-ter my mother was born (they knew full well that you do not raise *three* children in someone else's house), or that they were poised to move right after Ocie received his pharmacy degree from Illinois and right before Anna (my mother) was to enter elementary school. When they moved they bought; and what they bought was a house with a garage opening out onto an alley where you could trade with the ice man, the rags 'n' old iron man, the vegetable man; a house with a bare narrow yard that my wife and I later would have strained to cultivate into a restful city garden, but which was for them a functional rect-angle, suitable for burning trash at one end and for hanging clothes to dry at the other.

My grandparents bought their home from Germans who were master furniture makers, and who were slightly con-fused about why they had to sell and move no sooner than they had attained America—or better, why they had to move in order to maintain a certain citizenship in Chicago and America. Once the negotiations with the Germans were done, my grandparents finally had a Chicago house of their own, and two fine-crafted chairs in the bargain. I would like to think that the chairs, which are still in our family, were gifts of goodwill and housewarming. That's a good story. But the more significant one is the one my mother tells of the day, fifty years later, when my grandmother's eyes lit upon the chairs—after childrearing and householding, after Idlewild, after the death of Ocie—and said, "The chairs; is this *all* that is left?"

Our immediate neighbors to the north and south were, like Grandpa Burns and most everybody else I knew of that gener-ation, black postal workers, loyal both to the NAACP and to

the Republican party. To call their names and ours is like
sounding the roster of an NBA basketball team, or like whispering that of a Yale secret society of yore, for we all had
names like Collins and Kelly, Brown and Burns, York and
Bush. We knew the Kellys best: the parents were kind and jovial, their sons both brilliant and destined for extremes of
livelihood well beyond the steady rote of family, church, and
modest sinecure. One boy would prove gifted in mathematics
and earn advanced degrees in that field despite the major ob-
stacles the University of Chicago and the field itself would put
before him. The other son was equally smart but far more social, streetwise, and slick; he was "into" "politics." When I
saw him last he was dapper and clean, wearing a little mous-
tache and a good suit, and looking much too much like a
younger version of my father. Last I heard, he was about to
do time for some political "impropriety"—unusual but nonetheless possible in Chicago, especially if one has crossed the
wrong person in the ward or down at City Hall.

One neighbor was different from the rest of us. He had a big
car, possibly a boat, and when he came home from wherever he
worked he paraded around in "sport clothes," which told all
that he had *not* come home to fix something or burn trash or
stoke a furnace. I know he wasn't a postal worker, and I think
maybe he was a milkman: they seemed to have a whole lot of
style in the early 1950s, probably because they were delivering something in addition to milk. This man was bouncy,
happy, and possession-laden; that's why he bought a big Doberman pinscher, to help him protect his stash. This was seen
in the neighborhood as both a necessary act (hence, on some
level, to be forgiven) and an act of enormous hubris. Down at
Mr. Harris's barber shop, certain Negroes were saying things

like: "The next thing that nigger is goin' do is go to *France* and marry hisself the onliest *Chinese* woman he can find!"

This neighbor—let us call him Mr. Simms—loved his Doberman and his Doberman loved him back. They would go through all sorts of paramilitary exercises in Simms's version of the spare backyard we all had; grandstanding, really, quaking the neighbors who merely wanted to take down wash or wax a car—or simply sit a bit without a whole lot of foolishness going on. Another thing Simms and the dog did was to prance down Indiana Avenue to the newsstand every waking morning, scattering schoolchildren like leaves before a blower, and some adults, too. On the way back, much was the same, only now the Doberman delicately held the morning paper in his huge jaws while Simms smirked like a circus lion tamer.

This and other things Simms was up to clearly communicated the following: "I got me a Doberman, got him trained, mess with me and you got much Dog up your ass." People respected that; Simms's house was never approached, let alone robbed. But they were also incensed: for Simms's notion of the Protecting Dog was really that of the Harassing Dog, and that made Simms resemble a cracker sheriff more than anything else, and more than he, all vibrant in his sport clothes, ever realized. Perhaps that's why the following story was told and softly chuckled over many times in my boyhood.

One morning, Simms was late for work and hadn't time for the prance to and from the corner newsstand. He carefully explained this to the Doberman, in just the way serious dog owners talk to their animals, and then went off to work. When he came home that night to a dark house, Simms turned on a light and called out the dog's name, eager to see his best friend. But there was no response, no leaping, licking greeting. Simms went into another room, switched on a light; called. Nothing. Then he went into a third room, called, and before he could flick the light switch, the damn dog leapt from the dark into Simms's face, and bit Simms's ear off.

Just up the avenue from us was 58th Street, and the short stretch of 58th from Indiana Avenue east to Prairie to Calumet Avenue was an intense commercial district, brimming colorfully with every sort of store, business, and service. This was no doubt a result of the El stop at 58th—stores have always sprouted around train stops of any kind—right between Prairie and Calumet. Some of the stores were members of chains: there was a Walgreen's drugstore at 58th and Prairie, and the other drugstore a block away at Indiana, Silberman's, was a Rexall. But most of the enterprises were small, family or mom-and-pop affairs, with the usual breakdown of colored folk owning the barber and beauty shops, the rib joints, soul-food cafés, and more than a few of the bars, while the whites ran the pharmacies, the hardware, dry goods, and grocery stores, the meat and fish markets. A few of these places are as memorable to me as are the houses I have lived in.

Silberman's was a dark, narrow place that was rather uninviting. My father had his first office in the warren of rooms on the second floor. When Mr. Silberman retired, he sold his business to a black employee—that was a breakthrough and a great and good thing. The Walgreen's was ordinary enough but stood out then as now for me because of its lunch counter. It was there, usually while out on a romp with my mother or Aunt Marge, that I would be treated to a frothy milk shake or to my favorite out-of-the-house sandwich, grilled ham on raisin toast. The counter was run by two or three foxy brown-skin ladies, breathtaking even in uniforms and hairnets. Sisters like that naturally inspired a lot of fast talk—and Lord did they know how to dish it back. The banter at the lunch counter was funny, saucy, memorable; not as dirty as what came down at the barber shop, but still very adult.

When the lunch counter sit-ins began a few short years later in the South, and I watched the news films of the clubbings and draggings, the smearings of mustard and catsup, the burnings with lit cigarettes, my horror was matched only by my shame, the haunting shame of privilege. Nothing my elders ever said about privileges and "being grateful" cut half as deep as what I felt when I recognized that all I knew about lunch counters before 1958 was sweet talk and pretty ladies.

Harris's Barber Shop was on the south side of 58th, in the middle of a block not darkened by the girders of the El. It was the first of the several barber shops I've been destined to frequent where the talk is loud and quick and where an elder barber, usually the proprietor, can tell somebody to tone down ("Hey now, hey now, there are youngsters present," or, "Don't be talkin' 'bout *my* God that way!") and make it stick. Harris's was also typical in that the front of the shop displayed for sale shaving powders, pomades, and bacon rinds while the back had a curtain, behind which *something* to do with money was always going on. But what made Harris's a vintage, cut-from-the-true-mold ("dyed-in-the-wool"?) African American barber shop was that it always took ten hours to get a haircut because there were always forty Negroes ahead of you, even on a weekday morning.

A measure of my father's rise in the world came when he

decided he couldn't wait around Mr. Harris's—the amusements no longer offsetting the time lost—and found himself
a barber with whom he could make an *appointment*. But I, the
child, continued on at Harris's for several years more, perhaps
because the family still wanted to give him our trade, perhaps
because the few times my mother had taken me to a shop
nearer our home someone had been fresh with her (my mother
raged when a barber on 65th Street called her "baby"). No one
said this, but of course what was also going on was that my
haircuts were a means by which my parents kept in touch with
a life and neighborhood they were growing beyond. The same
could have been said of my churchgoing, which for stretches
of time was the only churchgoing being done.

Morry's Met Music Shop was east of the El, in a shadowed
block that may be dark in my mind for other reasons. The Met
was in those days the paragon of record shops, known for its
jazz (and written up accordingly in all the jazz magazines)
but, frankly, it had everything. My father and I would go in the
Met frequently at night, when the shop was something of a
hangout for jazz buffs, disc jockeys, and musicians. We'd grab
a few sides and then make our way through the smoke and
slick talk—trying hard not to jostle the clean dudes in cash-
mere overcoats and Florsheim's, the hopheads, or the Dizzy
Gillespie lookalikes in their berets—to one of the listening
booths lining the back wall. Crammed in a cubicle as small as
a telephone booth, we'd check out Ella, Sarah, the Duke, the
Count. I marveled at how my father could sometimes listen to
just one cut and then declare, "I *have* to have this jam!" I also
entertained myself by watching other people listening away
in their booths. Once I watched a fellow, who looked a lot like

Malcolm X, close his eyes and just take off for another world; Monk, I think, was doing that to him. But then he suddenly "woke up" and glared at me. I huddled closer to my father.

It was hard to leave the Met with just a record or two. But our purchases were that modest in the early days. Later, when my father began to make a little money, he would come home with a sack of take-out Chinese food from the Rumpus Room and five, maybe *ten*, records from the Met. What pleasure this brought him: he was playing Provider, and, indeed, what better provisions are there than Chinese food and a new stack of sides?

The Rumpus Room I also associate with good times with my mother. We would go there together before my sister was born on the Friday evenings when my father had a dinner meeting, perhaps after I had spent the afternoon waiting interminably for a haircut at Mr. Harris's or after we had had a short visit with Grandma and Grandpa around the corner on Indiana. I would invariably order beef and green peppers, my mom would order all those good things in dark oyster sauces which I wouldn't like until I was in high school. The Rumpus Room occupied a floor or two of what had obviously been an apartment building, and so there was a pronounced sense that that booth over there was in a former parlor, while that one there was in a former bedroom. The space emoted a sense of intimacy: soft jazz flowed through the speakers, couples leaned into each other, nice smells wafted from the kitchen; it was definitely Friday night. (Later, as a "college poet," I tried to commemorate all this with lines about "colored kitchens with Chinese cooks singing Lady Day.")

After dinner my mother and I sometimes went home and watched TV, which was no letdown for me since "Superman" was on and I was generally up for whatever was on since I could not watch TV during the school week. But other times we went to the "show," the movies, and saw some great stuff: *Shane, The African Queen, High Noon.* To this day, my mother and I talk about these films not in the context of television or videos or VCRs, but in that of strolling down the avenue, safely parking the car, and safely walking to a neighborhood theater to safely watch the film—not to mention safely going to the bathroom, if that was necessary.

The Rumpus Room was the restaurant I most had in mind when I blew up in 1972 at a now-distinguished colleague who chose then to suggest that my professed love of Chinese food indicated that my "blackness" was suspect. The Rumpus Room was as a much a part of the neighborhood as was any of the soul-food cafés, as the patronage of it readily attested. That colleague now resides in a northern city, and I hope she now has enough "experience" to change her view.

After I moved with my parents to our own house in Wood-lawn, I would return to the old neighborhood for haircuts and church. Church in the beginning was Good Shepherd—the Church of the Good Shepherd; later, around the age of nine or ten, I attended St. Edmund's, more formally known as St. Edmund's King & Martyr.

Good Shepherd had formed in the late 1920s right around the corner from my grandparents' home on Indiana Avenue. Grandma and Grandpa Burns had joined Good Shepherd right after moving to the neighborhood, and thus were members of the church from its inception. This always struck me as being curious since Good Shepherd is Congregationalist (now, United Church of Christ) and they were raised as Baptists and had been reinforced in that faith by their experiences at Tuskegee and Spelman. When I finally asked my mother about this, she explained that when her parents had come to Chicago, they had joined one of the famous, established Baptist churches, Olivet (they were among the five thousand black migrants who, according to James Grossman, joined Olivet between 1916 and 1919). But there had been a "falling out," something to do with "disrespect" at the time of my grandmother's sister's death. There may have been other reasons as well; at any rate, by the time I was born, Good Shepherd had been our church for almost twenty years. I was baptized there; it is the church to which the family returns to bury its dead, half wondering with no small degree of shame whether we can get home before getting mugged.

St. Edmund's is Episcopal and was my father's family's church. Indeed, my grandfather, Pa Step, had once been a member of the vestry: somewhere I have a photo of him almost glaring at the camera while at a board meeting, as I also have a photo of my father in his acolyte years, replete with cassock, surplice, and a puffy bow at his neck. In its early years, St. Edmund's had no church building; its services and meetings were held in rooms at the Wabash YMCA. By the 1950s, however, the parish had grown and prospered: in buildings once occupied by a Greek Orthodox church at 61st and Michigan, we had both a church and an elementary school.

St. Edmund's was not just Episcopal but high church, something that was mischievously explained as a trace of Father Martin's former days as a Roman Catholic. We had "bells and smells" in abundance, "exotic" images on the walls and in the architecture left over from the Greek Orthodox days, a choir that knew how to turn everybody on with its mix of

Bach and spirituals. We had the usual assemblage of trifling, cigarette-sneaking acolytes who (myself included) nonetheless showed up every Sunday and actually knew the mass. I was confirmed into the Episcopal Church at St. Edmund's in June in 1957; Grandma and Grandpa Burns gave me as a present the Bible I still have. I doubt they would have been so congratulatory if they had known that I had become, not so much through coaching as through sheer self-invention, a "confirmed" Anglo-Catholic, deeply suspicious of Roman Catholics and Protestants alike. My days with them at Good Shepherd were just that far behind me.

How this came about—and why I was abruptly moved from Good Shepherd to St. Edmund's in the first place—is something I have tried to piece together. The family line on this is that I was moved because the Sunday School at Good Shepherd was lousy, nonexistent. There is some truth to this: all I can remember of Good Shepherd's Sunday School is the softball games. This is because during one of those games I received the Revelation that left-handed people are supposed to bat from the *other* side of the plate. (With that knowledge, and a little practice, my batting average went up a zillion points.) At St. Edmund's, by contrast, those rooms in the elementary school were put to *use* on Sundays: we had Sunday School and homework, too.

The family line makes sense but is too pat an answer: What more were we leaving behind, what else were we moving to? Why would my mother leave the church of her youth and join St. Edmund's? Why did I accept the move so easily—is it possible that I may have even initiated it? Two stories seem to bear on this.

It was late on a wintry Saturday afternoon; Good Shep-

herd's Cub Scout pack, of which I was a member, was returning to the city after a joyous day of tobogganing out in the
western suburbs. Suddenly, the church bus pulled to the side
of the road right in front of a hamburger joint. We were going
to have a treat! Visions of milk shakes and french fries danced
in my head.

The scoutmaster got off the bus and went in to see if it
would be "all right." We all knew that "all right" wasn't simply about whether twenty Cub Scouts could enter the prem-
ises; it was about whether twenty black boys who claimed to
be Scouts should be let in. When the scoutmaster returned, he
spoke to us like this: "Now boys, we are going to go in here
and have ourselves a sandwich or something. But I can tell
you the people in there are none too pleased about all this.
Now, I needn't *remind* you that we are *not* on the South Side of
Chicago; this is *not* the chicken shack down the street from
your house—do you follow me? Good, so I needn't *remind* you
of how to BEHAVE, right? Am I right? OK; OK, now; let's go."
With that, we filed off the bus, hitting each other whenever
someone thought someone else was talking too loud.

The scene inside the hamburger place was not good. The
white cook and counterman (both of whom looked like they
should be sitting outside a filling station in Alabama) had instantly discovered, once deep into serving a bunch of Negroes,
how much that disgusted them. They scowled, they muttered,
they turned redder and redder by the minute. They half-
cooked the food, threw it on a plate, and hurled the plate in almost anyone's direction. They clearly wanted us to leave, but
in their fury constantly got the food orders wrong. We stayed,
waiting for our food, perhaps out of conviction but more likely
out of a kind of politeness (after all, the scoutmaster said, "BE-

HAVE"); witness for the first time in our lives to the spectacle of white men becoming unglued because of race. Then I said, loud enough and to no one—hence, to all: "Gee, this place has lousy service." No one replied; it was as if no one had heard me; but I had been heard.

When we got back on the bus, the scoutmaster started up: "You boys did fine in there. You all were real gentlemen. That is, all of you but one. I *asked* if you all knew how to behave, and you all said you did. Well, one of you *doesn't* know, and it's go- ing to be a long time before I take *any* of you anywhere again." I honestly wondered who this terrible person was; who had brought this down on the whole Scout pack? I tried to recall if someone had been loud in the restaurant, or otherwise cut the fool. Had anybody not used their silverware, their napkin? Had someone forgotten to say "please" or "thank you" or "yes sir"? I knew I hadn't.

But the bad egg was me, and the scoutmaster in effect both listed my sins and had them posted. I was told that I had made a bad situation worse, and that if I had held my tongue the sit- uation might have gotten better. I was told that I had endan- gered all of us, and had risked bringing violence upon us. I was told in pungent, quite vernacular terms that I knew nothing about "facing adversity with stoic dignity." I wanted to retort, "Bullshit." I wanted to remind everyone of who took us in that "cracker café" in the first place, instead of waiting until we were back in Chicago. I wanted to scream, but I said nothing, and not even a scream came out. I just sat and took it, my cheeks burning, my body shrinking, tucking itself into the folds of my winter parka, into the darkness enveloping the bus as day so gratefully became night.

Soon the bus cranked up, and we were on our way. No one

spoke to me, but I was consoled by the quickening certainty that we were no longer stalled in the suburbs and that being home was somehow going to happen. But we had an accident on the way home—a minor one—but accident enough. I am sure that there were some people on that bus who thought, "This would not have happened if Stepto hadn't queered the whole day for us." My thought was, "This is happening because we were so goddamn servile." We were a long time getting home.

After the episode in the suburbs, I was at best an indifferent Scout. I stopped doing the chores and projects that would earn me merit badges. I began to "play hooky" from Scout meetings, finding great pleasure in inventing places to go and in coercing a Scout or two to go with me. Once we rode to the end of the line of the commuter train I usually used merely to go from one point to another within Chicago; we went to "see what we could see" and were bitterly disappointed to sight nothing of interest. Another time we went downtown to the Loop to a coffee shop famous for its hamburgers—I see now that that was a brave attempt to undo or revise what had happened in the suburbs after tobogganing. I continued as a Scout because I had a few friends, liked the uniform, and had no idea of how to act upon the emotions washing over me. So, too, did I value being in a context where I had an identity: at Good Shepherd and even in the Cub Scouts I was "Miss Burns's grandchild." I thought that was my best merit badge, and I thought everybody thought so as well, but that was before the Sunday Grandma was hooted in the large basement room where Sunday School was held, and I had to witness the spectacle.

I was outside the church playing softball. It had been a

long time since any adult had suggested that Sunday School ought to foster something other than ball games, and so I was surprised when our game was broken up, and astonished by everything in the manner of the adult corraling us that told us we had been up to no good. When we arrived back inside the Sunday School area, there was much disarray and tension; the games and crafts which customarily occupied the youngsters not playing softball had been interrupted as well. People were grumbling: "What's going on?" "Who says this ain't a Sunday School?" "Sunday School these days ain't nothing but day care any way." "Somebody better wake up!" "I bet you one of them old-timey sisters from one of the guilds is behind this." "Who's that over there, passing out lessons?" "These children ain't going for none of that." "Who'd you say? Miss Burns? Oh, Lord, she done come back and doing it to us again."

The nut-brown woman with a determined look on her face, who was furiously slapping down lesson books (with Gentle Jesus on the cover) on top of board games and crayon drawings, was indeed "Miss Burns," my grandmother. I was mortified but also confused: I hated the way she was calling attention to herself (and hence, so I thought, to me); I hated what most everyone was saying about her (but knew that I had thought those things, especially those times when she abruptly turned off the television, because the cowboy movie I was watching was "too violent"). Matters did not improve during the excruciating remaining minutes of the Sunday School hour. Most of the youngsters were, I would say, disrespectfully silent; most of the erstwhile Sunday School teachers made it *look* like they were up to something pedagogical. Meanwhile, my grandmother, from her perch near the upright piano, sternly surveyed the scene, looking ever so much like your worst nightmare of a school principal or a plant manager.

Twenty minutes later, it was over, or almost over: Grandma had another card to play: she insisted that we revive the custom of ending Sunday School with a rousing rendition of "Onward, Christian Soldiers," which would end with all of us youngsters marching single-file out of the church building, gloriously into the sunshine. There was no recourse, especially after Grandma sat down at the upright and blanketed the room with hymnal chordings. The way out was simply the doorway through which we were to march, and march we did, though our clatter was hardly soldierlike. Once out into the sunshine, we wandered about, meandering in circles and half circles, trying to get a compass fix on our whereabouts. What I realized, once I got my bearings, was that I was in a zone of strange contradictions: I was outside the church when I was supposed to be inside; I was outside because my good Christian grandmother had in some real sense marched me outside; moreover, she had marched me outside in order to bring me, among others, inside—to make us true inhabitants of the church. It was all very confusing, wrenchingly so; I was quiet and subdued the rest of the day—I needfully got lost in a book, knowing well enough that this wasn't a good day for testing the limits on *The Lone Ranger.* All this occurred in the spring, in May I think. By the fall I was a regular in the pews at St. Edmund's.

I was last at Good Shepherd a few years ago for my Aunt Marge's funeral. It was blisteringly hot, so much so that when we found out to our great dismay that the air-conditioning in the church had broken down that afternoon, a few family members just stayed in the cool of the rented limousines until the service began. I was exceedingly uncomfortable but too restless to sit in a limo; I needed to explore what I could of the church, revisiting the vast basement room where the Cub Scouts had met, and from which I had marched to the strains of "Onward, Christian Soldiers" into another boyhood. I also needed to get a closer look at the children across the street, playing in the spray of an opened fire hydrant. Would they mind? Would they let me get close enough to see if I could see my child self in them? The heat bore in, I needed to get back in one of the limos, but I wanted more to walk around to the 57th Street side of the church to scrutinize the lot (really, the church's backyard) where I had played so many outdoor games, and learned to hit a softball, too. It was much as I thought it would be: narrow, spare, scruffy; I must have been a little tyke indeed to have once considered it a suitable space for serious ball games.

Then it occurred to me: you're already on 57th Street, maybe a quarter of the way to Grandma's house, why don't you walk down the street and around the corner and have a look? The appropriateness of this could not be disputed. To see the Burns house would be to see where our Washington Park life had begun sixty years before, and where my life had begun just after World War II. Even from across the street, I would be able to examine the little side entrance to the basement apartment where Marge and Rog had lived, and to watch the fading August sun burnish the second-floor window of what had been my parents' room, and later my room whenever I overnighted with my grandparents. I thought that all I was trying to pull together by roaming around instead of being in the limo would instantly coalesce once on Indiana Avenue, once reading the house numbers, "5722."

But I didn't go around the corner, even though I ventured seven or eight steps toward it. This was not because I thought I might miss the beginning of the service or because it was too hot to amble the streets. I didn't go because I was too well dressed and too light skinned; because I had a little money in my pocket and because I was wearing the nice watch my wife gave me for our twentieth anniversary. One side of my brain said, "Hey, my man, you're a brother—go on down to your grandmother's house and check it out." The other side said, "Don't fall for that romantic shit; this neighborhood has *changed*; walk two blocks and you're a dead man; the next funeral at Good Shepherd will be yours." Perhaps because a woman had been mugged at the wake the night before—she came running back into the church screaming, "My purse's been taken, he took my purse!" as if any of us could do anything about it—I listened to the second voice in my head. But I was angered by what was preventing me, a former child of those streets, from doing anything I wanted. So, too, was I angry about not being able to make the connection, which I thought to be the best possible connection, with the people, sites, and images that would put my life in order.

But I was wrong, for when I finally quit gazing down the street I wouldn't walk and entered the church, I found a feast for my eyes: the much older but still quite recognizable visage of the scoutmaster who had taken us tobogganing and later pilloried me some thirty-five years before. Family and friends from the year one broached conversation, and I believe I engaged them. But my eye was on Mr. B. Later I approached him, reminded him of how we knew each other, asked him how he had been, asked after his son, whom I remembered to be the Willie Mays of Cub Scouts. Mr. B. was very good at assisting the minister with the service, very short on everything else. He didn't remember me, and I almost got the feeling that he didn't remember the son of whom I had inquired.

This and the fact that, when it was time for me to speak, I was actually introduced as a *friend* of the family, and not as family, not as the firstborn nephew of the woman we were burying, made me aware not just of the corrosive forces of time, but also of what the young put in place to create chasms between the generations. I had wanted to be shut of Good Shepherd, and thirty-five years later I was faced with the evidence of how well I had succeeded.

Woodlawn

For some reason, I like to think that my parents and I moved to 6636 Minerva, in the Woodlawn area, just before my sister was born in 1953. But that wasn't the case. We were living on Minerva, for example, when Ma Step, father's mother, dropped dead of a heart attack right on State Street in the Loop, virtually in the vestibule of the State-Lake Theater— and that was in 1951. I was told of this by my father while we were in the tiny living room overlooking the street; as he held me in his arms and our bodies mournfully rocked, the plastic on the couch made creaking sounds; it was the sound of oars in oarlocks.

This means that the family's outrage over my grandfather's nearly instant second marriage (he married anew in less than two months) dates back to that time as well, and that all the sputterings and exclamations, as well as the hushed whisperings, were uttered on Minerva Avenue, not elsewhere. What the adults endlessly discussed was clear enough: Pa Step had disrespected Ma Step by remarrying so soon; more specifically, he was wrong to let everybody know in this way (everybody including Ma Step, somehow) that he had always had a woman "on the side." Others had choice words about the fact that the new woman was white, or, not only white but Roman Catholic. My father, the M.D., just six years out of medical school, liked to add for good measure that, on top of everything else, the new woman's father was an osteopath! (Only later could I comprehend the sense of betrayal buried in these exclamations.) For my part, I had nothing to contribute other than my amazement; I could scarcely believe that the grandfather who had given me my Mickey Mouse wristwatch was suddenly a villain.

So we lived on Minerva not from 1952 or '53 to 1958, but rather from 1949 or '50 onward, through virtually all of my school years before high school, not just through a few of them. These were the first years not under Grandma and Grandpa Burns's roof, and I missed them, missed the rides to school with Grandpa and his Irish coworker, Lawlor, missed singing "Frere Jacques" down in the basement with Grandma while "we" did the laundry. But communal living of some order did not end when we left the Burns house on Indiana Avenue, it just reconfigured itself. For when my parents bought the two-flat on Minerva, they did so in collaboration with Dorothy and Charlie Runner, whom they couldn't have known for very long, but with whom they instantly felt comfortable.

At the start, there were five or six of us; soon we numbered eight: Mom and Dad, Dorothy and Charlie, Dorothy's mother, Miss Walk (actually, Mrs. Walker), and the kids: me, Susan Runner, and my sister, Jan. People used to look at the names on the doorbells — Stepto, Runner, and Walker — and

strain to concoct witticisms about all the "feet" in the building (something that used to come back to me when in the
1970s I shared a Yale basement office with the historian
Al Raboteau and there were lame jokes about the "toes"
["teaus"?] down yonder). People also used to say, according
to my mother, "Ann, you're a fool to buy a building with
friends if you want to keep that friendship." But my folks and
the Runners went ahead, and when my mother died in 1991,
Dorothy could say, as she declared to me soon after the funeral, "Ann and I 'visited' every day for forty-five years." I
know that was the case; many was the time my mother would
disappear and be on the telephone, and then emerge, saying
something like, "You know, I just had to listen to all of
Dorothy's foolishness." This meant, of course, that Dorothy
had just had to listen to all of my mother's as well.

Driving around Woodlawn as I have recently, I am
moved—stricken, actually—by how the neighborhood has
been wasted, as if by war or disease. There are whole blocks of
vacant buildings—doorways sealed with sheet metal, upper-
story windows reduced to a few splintery members fanning
out toward street and sky, and there are whole blocks of rub-
ble, distracting in part because they tease you into wondering
if the prairie has once again been cleared to some purpose.
Upon second look, the destruction itself is not as arresting as
are the rearrangements of buildings and spaces, rendering
the familiar not just barren but strange. How amazing it is to
be driving along Woodlawn Avenue near 64th Street, and to
glance over and see Mount Carmel High School blocks away,
realizing all at once that you can see Mount Carmel from
Woodlawn now because there are no stores or businesses, no
houses or apartment buildings, to block your view; realizing,

too, that the whole idea that there should be stores and homes is predicated not upon some rosy notion of how things ought to be, but upon vivid memories of how things were, even in a neighborhood full of black folks.

How things were: it was, as the phrase goes, a built environment. At the corner of 63rd and Woodlawn, for example, where today you find only one building on one of the corners (a fortified mass of ghetto architecture, promising "discount" check-cashing), you once had real estate offices, a large pharmacy complete with a cafeteria, the main offices of a prosperous South Side bank (who would have thought its concrete pillars would fall?), and, nearby, jewelry stores, record and sheet music stores, a Chinese laundry and a French dry cleaners (such were the terms we freely used), a photography studio where a Mr. Stevens snapped cute portraits of children called "bunnygraphs." (Yes, there are "bunnygraphs" of me and my sister, she in ponytails and a party dress, me in a cowboy outfit, shamelessly waving six-shooters in the air.) There were at least three hotels: the Hayes, the Wedgewood Towers, the Southmoor—serving myriad clienteles (the Wedgewood was an oasis for Latin ballplayers; the Hayes, early on, filled with tiny white ladies fond of the tea room). There were at least four movie theaters: the Tivoli and the Lex, which I usually frequented at night with my mother; the Kimbark and the Stony, where us kids went for the Saturday matinees of cartoons, westerns, and monster flicks. There was a public library, a book-filled urban quiet space, the existence of which we simply took for granted.

The neighborhood was neither upscale nor (yet) downtrodden; it was simply full of people, black and white, bustling about, making a living, putting food on the table, seeking simple pleasures, finding respite from the summer heat in cool movie houses, restoring themselves after a trudge in the winter snow with a cup of coffee and maybe some lunch-counter banter. In short, there was activity, and while not all of the activity was wholesome or edifying (how well I remember the spectacle of watching a bloodied white man bounce along the sidewalk on his stomach after being thrown out of a bar), it mostly seemed to be about living, not dying—about getting on, not simply getting over. All this activity, this commerce in multiple senses of the term, made the streets safe, or safe enough. I am sure this was why I was allowed to walk most anywhere after, say, the age of six, and permitted to ride the buses, trolleys, and trains as soon as I was eight. People had places to go and things to do; and the urbanscape itself was more interesting than preying upon youngsters for kicks and small change.

All this presents itself when I think of how things changed, obviously for the next generation (before the age of ten, my older son was not only robbed but in the process dangled from a railroad bridge), but also for younger people within my own. Whereas I walked to school as early as the second grade, cutting a sprightly path through a mile of bustling urban life, neither my sister nor Susan Runner walked, and I think that had more to do with how things had changed than with gender. Later, when I rode the city buses, I did so for the company of schoolmates (the solitude of the walk suddenly palling by comparison), not because walking had become conspicuously dangerous. I don't think my sister or Susan, as girls, rode buses any more than they walked, nor were they expected to.

Their lives, our lives, were becoming suburbanized, even though we had hardly left the city.

Children who do not walk places, either in the city or countryside, do not see things well enough to study them, and generally miss out on the stimulations a walker navigates both toward and around—a shiny dime, a patch of poison ivy, a handbill for a gospel concert, deer tracks, the presser in the back of a cleaners who always waves when he sees you. Children who, for all the tedious contemporary reasons, never get to walk alone miss out on another thing, too: blazing the paths of one's own invention.

A few short years ago, after my wife and I suddenly tired of living half a block from an interstate and across from a lot blooming with trash, we forsook our city and moved out onto a couple of acres along a stream. One of the unanticipated pleasures for me was watching our younger son walk off to school. He would leave the house, cross the west yard, negotiate the rickety bridge across burbling water, and then turn back to the house for a glance of us, disheveled in our bathrobes, waving from a window. In the first days, Rafe would next descend to the county road and simply walk along the roads to school. But soon he invented a route, a path that took him through the woods, across the stream again (this time on a neighbor's bridge), back behind the house at the crossroads which long ago had been the tea room for the coaches plying between New Haven and the Naugatuck Valley, and then, after skirting the vegetable patches on the hill behind an old farmhouse, then, he was at school. How I envied him his path, and it was indeed his: there was no way that I, as an adult, could just take off across other people's bridges and gardens, no way that I could partake of the inner journeys Rafe's path inspired for him.

I can imagine Rafe's journeys for I had my own in my days in Woodlawn. Of all the walks—to school, to the library, to the movies, to the laundry—the one that haunts me, that seeps into dreams, is the one to the tiny grocery at 67th and Greenwood, mostly for the simple purchases mealmaking often demanded. My mother would say, "Bobby, we need milk/We need a stick of butter/Do you think that little store carries cinnamon?/Oh Lord, this calls for cheddar cheese," and I'd be out the door. There were other mom-and-pop stores to trade in, all about the same with the jars of penny candy and pig's feet, the coolers full of pop and Joe Louis milk, the skeleton set of boxes and cans. But I liked the store at Greenwood because, to get there, I had to take The Shortcut.

The Shortcut was, as my mother instantly told me whenever I took forty-five minutes to get a quart of milk, hardly that: it was the longest, most adventurous way I could think of to traverse three blocks. I started out from our back gate, and tumbled into the alley between Minerva and University avenues. If there was a stickball game in progress, I was good for an inning or two. Somehow or another, I got on to University, probably through somebody's backyard, and then made my way over to the Tot Lot, a pocket playground for toddlers. The swings and teeter-totters, though tiny, always looked like they needed my use. The back of the Tot Lot opened to the leg of the journey most responsible for my fantasies then, and my memories now: the wasteland behind the mortuary stone companies filled with the debris of finished orders and, as I recall, botched jobs.

Most of this yard looked like a roiling western river, like a treacherous green and brown stretch of the Colorado instantly frozen in marble by some sorcerer. The smooth, polished pieces were slippery, the rough chunks of granite cut at your skin and clothes. Nothing was ordered or stacked, everything jerked and heaved at crazy angles, a shoe could be pried off your foot by the claw two stones together made, and then tossed beneath a limbless angel. There was no path. Often, when I made my first foray into the rocks, my inner self would happily sit back, as if at the movies, and pleasurably take in the adventure unfolding: prospecting the Sierra Madres; sneaking up on the rustlers who stole my cattle; fleeing over the Alps with Lena Horne to escape the Nazis. But when I got to the middle of the debris, a fear almost oceanic in portion would take over, and I would ask: Why am I doing this? Can I get out of here? Can I get out alive?

The questions were a little ridiculous, and as melodramatic as was my final exit—my burst to Safety and into History—from the stony maze. The Shortcut was mostly a game, mostly something concocted from the plots of legend and Hollywood films. But it was about at least two other things as well: the mountain I'd scale to serve my mother; the desert I'd cross to get back home. Even now, when I'm tempted to read my tombstone stumblings as some sort of eerie anticipation of burying family across the street (four of us are there, along with Jesse Owens and Harold Washington and many Confederate soldiers), I hold off and return to what is incontrovertible: the long way home was the Shortcut to love.

My bedroom on Minerva was in the middle of the flat, halfway down the hall, right across from the bathroom. The sole window looked out upon the narrow gangway separating our building from Dr. Green's; all there was to see was the neatly tuckpointed brickface of Dr. Green's northern wall. I suppose I should have felt deprived of vistas, but I didn't: there was nature enough during the summers in Michigan, and even a grid of bricks, like the allegedly nondescript ceiling above your bed or favorite chair, yields pictures, images providing their own peculiar form of the familiar.

What was outside the window in abundance were noises, people noises, the sounds of people coming and going. My window was not, thank goodness, so low that I could directly see the passersby or that they could fully see me. What was on view was bobbing heads and bouncing caps; my sense of safety was oddly a matter of recognizing a head of hair, the tilt of a brim, the sway of either.

Though my room was bereft of much natural light, it was sunny in its glow, brightened further by a red linoleum floor. What I liked to do best was to build things: there was always a Revell model in progress on my worktable, sticky with glue. Lincoln Logs and Tinkertoy pieces were never far from reach. I stacked books and blocks to form the sides and decks of ships just large enough in the beam for me to squeeze aboard. There was much serious piloting, up the Great Lakes and the new St. Lawrence Seaway, across the Seven Seas.

I "gave up" my room to my sister when she was born in '53. It was weird to return and see a crib and changing table and neat stacks of gowns, blankets, and diapers where there had been the mess and trash of a seven-year-old boy's projects. I suppose I missed my old room, but not with the gnawing pain the childrearing books would predict. There was ample compensation to be had from moving into my father's study, and moving next to the kitchen.

The kitchen had the first floor I ever mopped, the first dishes I washed and dried; it began my full acquaintance with trash removal. It was also the kitchen in which I learned, from setting to clearing, how to mount holiday feasts and elaborate dinners for club meetings. After a club meeting, my mother and I would wash dishes for what seemed like hours, finding the teamwork, grinning when the end was in sight: "Just one more stack of plates, Bobby; one more tray of glasses; we're gettin' there." Sometimes, my mother would say at that point, "I can finish up now; you've been a big help," and I would glow. Usually, I stayed on to the end anyway, maybe for just another morsel of praise.

It is kitchen moments such as these which come to mind when I read books like Mary Mebane's *Mary*, her story of her black girlhood in North Carolina in the 1930s and '40s. In the early pages, before she begins to distrust what all the chores are preparing her for, Mebane rhapsodizes about working at her mother's side, gathering, canning, churning, laundering. Even ironing with Mama is a golden moment:

> After supper, Mama would start to iron on a big ironing board that had burned places at the end where the iron stood. I couldn't lift the real heavy iron, but she would let me have the small iron and I would push it up and down a handkerchief or a pair of socks, glad to be a woman like Mama.

I know a lot about this, about working side by side with a grandmother, a mother, or a housekeeper, doing the most domestic of chores, taking pride in the work, sharing standards, agreeing with a wink on what is a good corner to cut; glad for

BLUE AS THE LAKE

the company. But of course, I've never been able to say of this, "glad to be a woman like Mama."

My mother and I never talked about this directly, precisely because it was intolerable to each of us, perhaps for different reasons, to think that what we had forged in the kitchen and which gave us succor was less than real because I was a boy. We got at it differently, elliptically. When my mother felt good, even triumphant, about her training of me, she would crow, "Who said you can't have as much fun raising boys as girls?" and make sure I heard her. But on another day, she would tell me, "You're too soft to be a lawyer" (I had mentioned once, while we were folding clothes, a curiosity about lawyering), and we would stop for a beat and look at each other, our eyebeams bound in the hope that no one would next say something to be regretted.

Thus did we start, from the Woodlawn days, down the path of our particular intimacy. My mother's project of me was plainly one of turning the survival lessons so anxiously imparted to her by her mother during the Depression into chores which would ensure that I wouldn't be another "Milkman Dead," another unskilled and shiftless child of privilege. (How well I remember how she would push our housekeeper away from some task, reminding her, "This is Bobby's job.") But the project was never that simple; other matters intruded: she had to wonder what sort of "man-child" she was raising (in the 1950s, no less); I was forced to ask if I was a "Mama's Boy" (and if that was a problem). Both of us had to acknowledge, though we didn't before my senior year of high school and then most inarticulately, that what had seemed to be my training in householding had been, so ardently, our mutual quest for companionship.

· 68 ·

Woodlawn was the neighborhood of my youth most abuzz
with children at play. Every day of good weather, our block
looked like a carnival or a track meet: if you got off the bus at
67th and started walking home, you had to duck baseballs,
freeze to avoid charging halfbacks, swear with your eyes that
you wouldn't let on where hide-and-seekers were hiding, skirt
a wide circle around the rope jumpers, and by all means do
nothing that could be construed as spoiling the "aim" of the
big boys pitching pennies ("You know, I could have won that
if you hadn't brought your sorry ass over here . . ."). The scene
was like the urbanscapes by black painters like Jacob Lawrence and Archibald Motley, just as animated, jazzy, just as vibrant in hue. It seems remarkable now that we played so freely
and safely into the twilight, fearing only the dismays of
athletic defeats—and the cruelties children havoc upon each
other.

The first time or two I went to play I timidly stood to the
side and watched, now and then retrieving an errant ball in
the hope that I would be rewarded with an invitation to join
in. Fat chance. When I finally asked to play, there was much
muttering and sputtering before a big brown boy named Hudson stepped forward and said, "No." When I complained,
"How come?" Hudson stepped toward me again and, with a
cock of his head, said, "'Cause you white." Angrily, without an
ounce of style, I shrieked, "I am not white!" Hudson then came
a little closer, cocked his head again, and told me, "Well, if you
ain't white, your momma sure got a pink ass." The guffaws
from the rest of the kids followed me half the way home.

Besides being shocked and humiliated, I was impressed.
These kids were for real; they played the dozens; they got up

in your face. They were boys with names like Buster and Bishop and Hudson, and girls with ordinary names but whose daughters and daughters' daughters would have all the "L" names from LaJuanita to LaToya. Buster told epic stories of how his father would come home, strip him, and beat him. Annie knew how to archly ask, "When he stripped you, didn't he see your Thing?" All this was a wonder and a revelation to me; I didn't even know any adults who talked this kind of high octane trash.

I finally got in the game when I caught the ball. The ball sailed over someone's head one day, and I caught it. Then I did it again, and I was in. My abilities did not endear me to everyone: Harry Stevens once came after me with a baseball bat after I caught his screaming line drive, robbing him of a triple. But there was no question of my playing. The older boys, perhaps because we were growing up in the era of the Cold War and a certain kind of comic book, took to calling me their Secret Weapon. We would barnstorm the neighborhood, challenging teams in the sandlots and schoolyards, and they would put me in short center or right field. There was always one boy, in the first inning or so, who would deliberately slam the ball my way and start his home run trot. When I caught it, my teammates would hoot, do some sort of 1950s high five, and wave at the pissed-off batter. For fear of death or worse (I still had to walk the streets), I didn't join in the antics. But I was pleased, thrilled in every fiber behind my mask of youthful wonder.

While I was allowed on the field (whether the "field" be a schoolyard, a vacant lot, or the alley), I rarely could bat, never if there were men on base. In such situations, one of the bigger boys would push me aside, not brutally but in a businesslike way, saying, as he stalked to the plate, "I'm gonna take care of this!" And usually he did.

One hot summer day, a bunch of us strolled down 67th to the grocery store near Greenwood to buy cold drinks. On the way home, we got involved in a pickup softball game in the vacant lot bumping against the yard full of broken, discarded tombstones, directly across the street from the mausoleum where I now must go to visit my mother. At one point, with a man on base, I actually got to bat, hit a sharp single, and stretched it into a double when the ball rattled around in the shards of cemetery marble, eluding for a jot the eager fielder. As I stood on second base, I swelled with pride, and looked over for the acclaim of my teammates, my neighbors. I wanted to hear the hoots, to see the high fives raised before when I had caught a ball raised now for a new job well done. What I saw instead was a big boy named Leroy loft my cold soda in a kind of exaggerated toast before, with great smacking of lips, he drained it dry.

Twenty years later, my mother called to tell me that Leroy had died in an auto accident, his car missing a turn and plunging deep into a lake. I made noises of regret, but never said I was sorry.

We moved out of Woodlawn in 1958, less than ten years after moving in. If we hadn't been living in a stable block, in which colored folk actually competed for Best Lawn, Best Tulips, Best Storm Windows, we might have realized how quickly the neighborhood was deteriorating and moved sooner. Of course, there were signs: apartment buildings were being

carved into the notorious kitchenettes Gwendolyn Brooks
writes of, housing hundreds, not the intended tens of people;
and, as if afloat, they drifted closer and closer. With the invention of that sort of middle passage, the schools bulged and
went on double shifts, and the businesses that stayed started
to look uniformly like pawn shops—same junk, same bars and
locks, same obscene ability to meet a person's wants but not a
family's needs. And there were the signs children tend to pick
up on first: the new hostilities from the mom-and-pop mer-
chants, the spectacular dangers now awaiting at the Boy's
Club, the bus rides home from school that suddenly didn't include white classmates anymore—they had disappeared to
parts of the city not just unheard of but unpronounceable.

Despite clear memories of these things, I was nevertheless
shocked to read in Nicholas Lemann's *The Promised Land* that
the "tide was running out" of Woodlawn long before the
1960s, before gangs like the battalion-sized Blackstone Rang-
ers were all the neighborhood would be known for. Lemann
reports that even Saul Alinsky, the miracle-working community organizer (and father of David, my classmate), had given
up on Woodlawn in the late fifties, and went to work there
only to placate his most powerful backer, the Catholic Arch-
bishop. We were moving, but spoke very little of Woodlawn in
these terms. It wasn't just because our block was "good." It
was because we were moving to something, not from something, with all of the emotional energy focused on the "to." Basically the choices were these: you could move to Hyde Park
and be near your school and the shops where you traded and
maybe participate as you were inclined in that neighborhood's
experiments with integrated living, or you could move further

south and west and pursue something equally elusive—the creation of a middle-class black community that successfully stymied the entrepreneurial schemes of whites and blacks alike and stayed middle class. In short, you could risk living in the one nearly hospitable white neighborhood or you could risk living in a black suburb that was a viable option precisely because it was not a true suburb but instead an enclave within the city's reaches. The Runners, with whom we lived almost communally in Woodlawn, went to Hyde Park, Dorothy's status as a University of Chicago faculty member helping them buy one of the new townhouses near 55th Street. We went the other route, and found our suburb in Chatham, an area then difficult to describe except in terms of how quickly certain classes of white people left, and who was left when the dust cleared (for starters, us, Ernie Banks, and a very young Jennifer Beals).

We were moving on up to a yellow brick house of Georgian style on a corner lot with lawns and trees. There were landscape amenities such as an underground sprinkling system, which was handy but also strangely discomforting—you could come out with the tool that worked the pipes and get the system nicely going and attract a whole small crowd of Negroes. Some were amazed, some thought you were showing off, pitifully few only thought you were watering the grass. Being on a corner we were also at a crossroads; at the center of the crossroads was a circular planter which the city actually impressively festooned each May. Such unheard-of attentions from the city told us we were in a new and strange place. Another expression of this was that, though near a bus-line, we were at the end of the line. Having a bus turn around to go back where it came from before it lets you off particularizes not just your stop but where you live: even if miles of city still sprawl about you, you have been outposted; you experience too occasionally the ambiguities of being the last person left off, the only person walking away.

Our departure from Woodlawn was thus our move to suburbia. While there was still a lot of city left, especially to the west, while there were friends as close as a mile away, while being at the end of the busline was far better than being miles away from the end of the line, we were isolating ourselves in ways that we had to live through in order to know and face. I think here especially of my mother, who had been willing to stay home and raise kids after realizing what a whipping had been put on her during a decade of teaching in some of Chicago's toughest schools. But she had not stayed home to become Suburban Mom, which was another kind of whipping for a woman of her sensibilities.

A family that has always lived communally, either with relatives or close friends, can't always imagine what awaits them in a home of their own. No matter how many years deep you are into a marriage and childrearing, you are doing something new: you are beginning again, maybe beginning for the first time. Did my parents sense this beginning? Did they sit in the kitchen and talk of these things after the children had gone to bed? Of course, I don't know. But I know of my sense of beginning, out there. I remember the early risings to do chores and get places, and the late evenings that were late because you had to commute back to where you were from from where you had to go. I remember my mother driving hither and yon, carting us kids, sometimes making two or three daily trips to the neighborhoods where everything in our lives actually occurred. I remember sometimes insisting on taking the bus and being the last person on a bus in winter, my feet immersed in the black slush slimeing the aisles. No matter how much you joked with the driver, there was still the whirling about-face of the bus to contend with, still the cold walk home.

II

Migrations

Up to Baltimore

The train was rolling north out of Raleigh, North Carolina, easing into a rhythm made for low-sweat tap dancing. It was December, and there were just enough days between the end of classes at St. Augustine's and Christmas for Grace Williams to visit her aunts in Baltimore. The trip had been proposed by her aunts (her mother Blanche's two younger sisters) and paid for by Aunt Grace, for whom Grace had been named. The aunts had hit upon the trip as a special, festive way to honor Grace's sixteenth birthday while launching the holiday season as well. But Grace knew other things were afoot: there had been the sudden flurry of notes to her mother; there had been all the whisperings between the younger sisters when they had visited the summer before. Grace sensed that they were making a project of her, especially now that she was sixteen; this trip had something to do with that.

The coach car Grace rode in was cool; there was nothing warm about the air or the winter-faint light barely flickering in the mottled coach windows. Yet Grace was warm and getting uncomfortably so. She picked at the lint on her coat. She shifted her purse from her thigh to her side then to her lap. A soft whirring sound registered: her clothes were humming and buzzing as she tried to get comfortable. She thought of opening her coat, for just a little air, a little less confinement. But she stopped her fingers inches short of the buttons; intuitively she knew that ladies do not open their coats.

This lady business: it had to do with her parochial schooling, with her turning sixteen, and with the aunts in Baltimore, fussing with their gloves, anticipating Grace's train. In the here and now, however, it had to do with not reacting to what seemed to be the overtures from that soldier a few seat benches away. Yes, the soldier's ever so slight smiles, the milliseconds of his glancing her way, were polite, gallant. But they were overtures, beckonings to acquaintance. "Oh, Lord," she thought, "this is what Momma had been talking to me about in the train station just before I left."

But it hadn't exactly been a talking-to that Blanche thrust upon her daughter: it had been a geometry of signs; not the broad, exaggerated sweeps of arm and leg we see in sports, but a signal vocabulary contained quite close to the body, stretching rarely beyond the rectangle configured between bosom and waist and the normal reach, left and right, of hands of good manners. Blanche could "say" a great deal with those fast fingers of hers—she had been deaf since 1883 when fever and meningitis had almost wiped out more than just her hearing—and if her back were toward you you often could not detect that those fingers, so hummingbird-like in their quickness, were doing anything at all. Grace knew all this but had nonetheless been mortified during the last minutes with

Blanche in the station. "Why is Momma doing this now? Why do we have to go over this lady thing again? Why didn't she do this in the taxicab instead of in front of all these people?"

Grace got nicely distracted remembering her mother, and remembering too that she and Blanche were all that was left of the family now that her father and brother had died. Here she was, sixteen and living alone with a deaf woman in the cramped rooms the School for the Deaf provided them (her late father had supervised the school's colored division). She yearned for company, for conversation, for gaiety. Yes, Baltimore; even Baltimore with the prissy aunts would do. Yes, thank you, I'm coming. I'm coming for sure.

Grace was so consumed with her fretting and fuming that she jumped when the soldier shook his newspaper and began whapping it into a new fold. She had momentarily forgotten him. But now she jumped and, startled, looked right at him. He lowered his paper in an easy curve, met her gaze, and smiled. "Oh Father," she said, "light eyes. This colored soldier boy messing with me has got light eyes." Grace put her gaze back where it should have been, taking in everything and nothing. She straightened her clothes. She double-checked her tickets and itinerary. Then she sighed a careful little undercover sigh. That seemed OK.

Grace's train was due soon in Washington, D. C., the end of the line. She was a little nervous about changing trains, about crossing the station and finding the right train to Baltimore. She hadn't done it alone before. But now she was strangely glad she had to negotiate this. Changing trains meant she could get away from this soldier. It meant she could compose herself before encountering Aunt Grace and Aunt Ruth. It meant that she could begin to tell herself that all the heat and eye contact with the light-eyed soldier boy hadn't happened.

Everything went well enough in Union Station in Washington. Indeed, that hour in Union Station proved to be one of the first clarifying moments when the adolescent Grace discovered that she was in public both so *distrait* and so attractive that the best sort of men would come to her aid. The Red Cap who saw her struggling with her bags and squinting at train postings, lurching in the process in five different directions, saw a daughter in need, and with an avuncular smile eased to Grace's aid. She was in safe hands when he steered her toward her next train, and also when he directed her to a water fountain in a hidden alcove, a fountain providing the coolest, most refreshing water of which colored people could drink in the Station.

Grace drank at the fountain, letting a little of the water spill about her cheeks, her handkerchief absorbing the moist residue. Then she surged toward her train, pressing a coin upon the Red Cap, determined not just to meet her train but also to consider seriously her Baltimore possibilities. Her aunts were tedious, but they offered a way out of narrow, suffocating Raleigh. Most of the people there were still nice enough to her and to Blanche. But in the years since her father's death, there had been more than few hints that people would forget who her father had been and see only instead a penniless girl who could have been a catch.

Clearheaded, Grace entered the train for Baltimore, admiring that it was just a bit cleaner. That supported all her fantasies, in 1917, about how all things were demonstrably better once one ventured north. In addition to her purse and bags, she was carrying flowers now, fresh from the pretty booth in the Washington station. Grace couldn't quite remember whether flowers were for people getting off trains or for the people meeting trains, but these flowers were nice, and maybe if she gave them to her aunts the visit would start in just the right, pleasant way.

Suddenly, someone sat next to her. Grace scooped up the flowers, shocked that they almost got trampled. Hugging them to her bosom, she stared out the window, blindly taking in the odd house, the odd meager business, dotting the landscape. Curiously enough, staring out the window actually helped Grace focus upon who was suddenly at her side: it was the soldier from the other train, whapping his newspaper again, clearing his throat, smelling of mints.

Long minutes, clusters of them, marched by, and then the soldier spoke, as Grace knew and dreaded he would. "This train is much cleaner than the other one," he said breezily. "Too bad I am only going as far as Baltimore. I like a clean train. How far are you going?" Grace thought about not replying. She knew her mother wouldn't want her to reply. But then she found herself staring at the back of the seat before her and, with a strange sigh, whispering, "I am going to Baltimore, too." The soldier half-turned in his seat as if to marvel at this coincidence, hoping Grace might do the same, but she didn't. She kept staring straight ahead.

"Actually," the soldier continued, "I'm just getting off the train at Baltimore. I'm going down to Camp Meade, near Annapolis. Have you ever been down to Annapolis?" Grace shook her head to tell him she had not. "Pretty town, right on the water," the soldier declared.

Grace wasn't curious about Annapolis and made no response. Her seat partner was undeterred. "Camp Meade," he almost barked, "Camp Meade is home to the 167th Field Artillery Brigade, as fine a brigade of colored soldiers as ever walked the earth!" Listening, Grace couldn't help but turn her head a little. "I'm a corporal in a regiment of the 167th, the 351st regiment; have you heard of us?" Grace of course had not. "Well, you will hear of us, especially after we get our guns a-smokin' and blow 'Bill Kaiser' sky high!"

Instantly, Grace recoiled, the shudder of the flowers in her hands recording her agitation. The easygoing soldier immediately sensed his mistake and sought to make some repair. "Oh Miss, I'm sorry," he began. "You know how it is; being around soldiers you just fall into some rough talk. All I was trying to say is that we are a bunch of fine boys, Pittsburgh boys from the same mills, the same ball teams, and we now got a chance to do more in this War than clean latrines and valet officers. We are artillery. If we can get to the front in France, we're going to make good!"

Grace didn't know what to say, but the fact that she now turned toward the soldier, as he had previously wheeled toward her, was statement enough. Sensing Grace's new presence, and the possibility that their eyes might meet like they had before, the soldier pressed on with his conversation. "I know I'm a stranger, and you're not supposed to be talking with strangers. I know if I had put my sister on this train, the last thing I would have said to her would have been, 'Don't be talking with any strange men—especially, any of them soldier boys.'" Grace smiled at that. "So, let me try to fix things."

Assured as only young men are that all they have to do is introduce themselves, the soldier grinned and started in. "I am Corporal Robert L. Steptoe of the 351st Field Artillery;

we really are at Camp Meade; I really am from Pittsburgh. I am an honorable young man, and your daddy can investigate me any day he wants and find this to be true." Grace heard this and thought first of how she didn't have a daddy anymore. But then she thought, what is this? This boy is talking like I am going to see him again.

The conductor came through the coach bellowing that Baltimore was nigh, ten minutes at most. With great studious inattention to her seatmate, Grace began to gather her belongings. Her purse at this point was almost next to the corporal's newspaper; reaching for it, she couldn't help but notice that the newspaper was a copy of the Pittsburgh *Courier.* "Well," she thought, "maybe this soldier really is from Pittsburgh." Rightly or not, Grace relaxed a little, her movements taking on a fluidity, a grace, they hadn't had before when she was fearful. When the corporal asked if he could help her with her bags to the platform, Grace said yes with both her words and her eyes.

Aunt Grace and Aunt Ruth were perhaps fifty feet away when Grace and the corporal stepped down to the platform. Each was well-dressed in a tailored way with just the right accessories. Aunt Ruth maybe had the nicer hat, but Aunt Grace was wearing fur and looked superbly put together. While their attire was an easy read—you knew these were proper colored ladies from some neighborhood like Druid Park (and that was precisely where they resided)—the expressions on their faces were more difficult to fathom. Grace was puzzled at first, but only for an instant: the soldier loping beside her, carrying her bags, was the issue, the problem. Stupidly, she had complicated what was supposed to be her grand arrival to Baltimore.

Instinctively, Grace ran ahead toward her aunts, to hug them of course, but also to widen the space between her and the smiling corporal—a distance which she hoped he had the good sense to maintain. Grace jumped into the embraces of her aunts; kisses pressed splashes of warmth on to winter-chilled faces; blissfully, Grace nuzzled in the fur about Aunt Grace's still youthful neck. Perhaps with a sense of who had paid for the trip, Grace gave the flowers to Aunt Grace. Then Aunt Grace said, "Aren't you going to introduce us to the young soldier with your bags?" Grace fell away from her aunt's arms, half turning toward the corporal. She beckoned him, finding herself amazed that she was doing so. He strolled forward.

Grace began: "This is Corporal . . ." Filling the pause she didn't mean to create, he said, "Corporal Steptoe; Robert Steptoe; from Pittsburgh." Grace anxiously looked into her aunts' eyes but saw nothing forthcoming. With a lot less bravado than he exhibited on the train, Robert Steptoe, now hat in hand, went on. "I am on my way to Camp Meade; I am with the 351st Field Artillery Regiment. I guess you may have heard that they transferred a bunch of us last month from Camp Lee to Camp Meade. It was in the colored newspapers. We had been assigned to a service battalion down there in Virginia; you know, dig ditches, clean latrines. But now we are field artillery; now we got a chance to prove ourselves."

Before the aunts could say anything, a man burst into the circle. "Yes, I read about that," he declared, taking center stage. "Read about that in the *Afro-American*. So, you are one of those Pittsburgh boys creating all the havoc down at Camp Meade?"

With that, William McCard appeared, directing a Red Cap to relieve Corporal Steptoe of Grace's bags. William McCard was Aunt Grace's husband. A Baltimore lawyer, a civic mover-and-shaker, a founding member (along with his physician brother) of the local Boulé, William was conspicuously the best catch any of the Wilkins sisters had managed. He was also the kind of well-dressed colored man who filled Corporal Steptoe with raging competitiveness—and surging unease.

Genially, McCard stepped forward to the soldier. "Hey," he said, "just kidding." Corporal Steptoe wasn't quite convinced. "Let's get those bags on the cart," McCard continued. "It looks like Grace has packed for a year not a week!" McCard winked at his niece. Turning, he extended his hand and with a handshake let the soldier know that he and the ladies were leaving.

Corporal Steptoe wanted to shake Grace's hand, too, but everything about these people told him that was impossible. He had to settle for just another look of her, another hope that she would return his gaze. "Goodbye," he said. "Yes, good-bye," chimed McCard, intruding before Grace could open her mouth. "And Merry Christmas, too."

Perhaps especially because he was in the Army, Corporal Steptoe knew he had been dismissed. Grabbing his duffle, he strode off in search of the military bus to Camp Meade, mindful of where he was going yet full of a welter of thoughts about Grace and her people and people like them in Pittsburgh. Moments later, while they were still negotiating their way out of the station, Aunt Ruth broke through the giddy family chatter and spoke for the first time. "Light eyes," she said. "Nothing but trouble." Aunt Grace smirked and did a little stutter step;

McCard mimicked her and started chortling. Young Grace felt the heat rise again in her cheeks.

Strictly by chance, Grace and Robert saw each other again the very next Friday evening. One of the civic duties Aunt Grace and Aunt Ruth performed was to help host socials at the Baltimore WCCS (War Camp Community Service) clubroom for the colored soldiers from Camp Meade. The last social of the year was scheduled for the Friday of Grace's visit, and as it was to be a special, holiday party, the aunts urged Grace into a party dress and brought her along. In truth, they needed her help with the last-minute decorations, and later, with serving refreshments. But they were also thinking that it was never too soon to introduce their young niece to some of the virtuous activities that would occupy her when, say, she was suitably married.

Aunt Ruth froze in her tracks when she saw Robert Steptoe breeze in the door, snapping his head right and left. "Oh my," she whispered.

"What? What is it?" said Aunt Grace, spinning about. Then she too spied Robert. Aunt Ruth whispered again: "Do you think he knew Grace would be here?" "How could he," replied Aunt Grace, "when we invited her to come along just last night?" "Do you think he will see her?" Aunt Ruth was sounding anxious.

Aunt Grace sighed, "How is he going to miss a pretty girl in a pretty dress serving punch?" Ruth shot back, "Do you think Grace can handle this?"

Aunt Grace laughed softly. Her sister's questions reminded her of their Minnesota girlhood together, when, with Mae grown and off to Chicago and with Blanche away in Faribault at the School for the Deaf, she was big sister and Ruth was baby sister. Turning to Ruth, leaning into her, Aunt Grace purred, "The question is, can *you* handle this?" Ruth straightened, narrowing her eyes with annoyance. In a huff, she went searching for cake forks, brushing by her niece as she did, as if to make sure she were still intact.

Robert Steptoe's quick scanning of the party room had taken in everything he wanted to know, and one lovely surprise as well. Yes, the pretty girl by the punch bowl was the girl from the train. He was rivetted by the sight of her sweet figure, which her coat had cloaked before. And yes, as he suspected, not too far away, hovering, were the two matrons he had met on the train platform whom he remembered to be the girl's aunts. Though fatherless and a bit adrift, Robert had occasionally moved about in Pittsburgh's colored society, his charm and light skin having opened some doors, if not others. He thus had had a social education, chiefly because he had desired one, and had a keen sense of the pecking order that applied most anywhere. It was one thing, he knew, to get invited to socials like this one, and quite another thing to be of the echelon that, with varying degrees of civic-mindedness, planned and paid for them, and hosted them, too. In another setting, the assignment of a girl to a punch bowl would have been emblematic of her need for work, her servitude. But here, for Robert, Grace's tasks transformed her into a princess, a charming lass of the near-but-elusive classes. In his fantasies, fueled now by the remembered glint of McCard's cuff links and the lush, snow-wet smell of Aunt Grace's furs, Grace was a young woman who, if you got a little closer as he planned to do, would faintly smell of spices, of perfumes, and money.

One of the aunts (he never bothered to get them straight)

was watching Robert watch Grace. That in itself confirmed that he was going to have to consider carefully how and when to approach her. He knew the "when" was not now, and was glad to see Jim Haney from his regiment hailing him. Robert liked Jim Haney; they had a lot in common. Both men were from Pittsburgh; both had finished high school and both were seething about the job prospects for colored men like them who were determined not to follow their fathers into the most dangerous jobs in the mills. Jim used to say, "I finished high school so that I could become a night watchman??" That pretty much said it all. Then the War came and the announcement that a colored regiment from western Pennsylvania was being formed, and that for this regiment the Army wanted high school graduates and colored men with some college. Robert and Jim and men like them scarcely could believe their ears. They signed up in a minute. Now, Jim and Robert talked all the time about going into radio together when they got back from "whipping the Hun." Radio? Radio?? The War was rekindling Dreams.

When Grace ladled the last of the punch out of the vast bowl she cradled it in her arms and took it out to the kitchen. Her aunts had already shown her where the various juices were and she set about replenishing the bowl. Something told her someone else was in the room, but before that sensation became a fear she heard "Hello" from a voice she knew but couldn't absolutely place. Turning, she saw a man in uniform. "Corporal Steptoe!" "Ah, you remember my name—a good sign!" he grinned. "But I want you to call me Robert, Bobby, even." Grace did not know what to say or do. She stood frozen to the spot, her mouth still open in surprise. "Listen," he urged, "I don't have a lot of time to say what I want to say, and

I don't want some testy conversation with one of your aunts who might think the worst of me being out here in the kitchen with you. Please put that jug of juice down."

Grace had forgotten about the juice. Now that it rematerialized it seemed heavy. She slid it to the counter. With a glance at the door, Robert started in. "Look, with the War, with our training almost done, I might not see you again. But I want to see you again. I want to go off with only you on my mind and only you in my heart, and I want to dream of you when I need the sweetest of dreams. And I want to come back and see you again. And again. Tell me your address so I can write." Grace told him. "If you don't hear from me," he began again, "it's only because the War is in my way. Is there a place in Raleigh, a drugstore or something, that carries the colored newspapers?" Grace whispered, "Yes." "Do they carry the Pittsburgh *Courier*?" Whispering again, Grace said, "I'm not sure; I think so." Sensing the elapse of time, knowing that others needed items in the kitchen, too, Robert rushed to complete his message. "The *Courier* is following the regiment. Look for news of me there. And I will be writing. I'll be back for you. So long, darling."

With certain, full-blown gallantry, Robert took up Grace's hand and kissed it for seconds on end. She wondered if this was really happening. Then he dashed out the service entrance, almost crashing into the kitchen debris that lay between the kitchen and the street.

It was a simple business to return to the social through the main doors of the building. Jim Haney spotted Robert first. "Where you been, Bob, I thought we were having a conversation?" Corporal Steptoe chuckled and put his arm around the shoulder of his buddy. "Jim, old boy, I've been dreaming dreams and putting a few things in place. And I'm not talking now about radio." No fool, Jim smiled and said to himself, "Step is messin' with some woman."

Corporal Steptoe and the rest of his regiment did not leave the States for Europe for another six months. Even so, there never was a respite, a break in the grueling round-the-clock training, in which he could dare to travel to Raleigh and see Grace and get back by curfew. *Dare* applied to the situation in other ways as well: despite the smooth talk, however earnest it actually was, how could he dare to get off a train in Raleigh and then hang about the schoolyard, or ring Grace's mother's doorbell, in quest of a moment with a properly raised girl still in her teens? That was a dilemma that the corporal, at age twenty-three, had no idea of how to face. The War and the training for it gave him a cover: he could truthfully say he only had time for postcards, postcards artfully crafted to keep Grace warm and aflutter while raising no concern for mother Blanche. Indeed, Blanche, who had her own concerns, merely thought it nice that a young man Grace had met while in the society of her sisters wrote occasionally to say hello.

It is surprising that Corporal Steptoe managed those few postcards given how the Army was severely on his case, and those of all the Pittsburgh soldiers. William McCard might have said when he met the Corporal that he was "just kidding" about the trouble the Pittsburgh soldiers were creating, but that was only because he saw no point in referring to the ugly side of a situation that had almost ignited into violence. As an educated man, McCard no doubt sympathized with the Pittsburgh soldiers. And yet, as a colored man of Baltimore and of Maryland, he could easily see the point of view of the colored

Maryland soldiers who were being bumped out of jobs and possible promotions by the cocky new arrivals from Pennsylvania. That this was happening to Maryland boys in Maryland, right in a Maryland Army camp, right in front of their daddies and mommas, especially their mommas, was too much for the locals to bear.

This is how Robert Steptoe told the tale of Camp Lee and Camp Meade—once he returned from the War, once he invented himself as Robert *Stepto*, once he needed to tell his Army stories:

I'd been working as a porter, sometimes as a machinist when I could find the work, when the War broke out and the Army came to Pittsburgh recruiting colored boys. Oh, it wasn't like later, when Lieutenant Tootle came to town and signed up hundreds of boys from the Hill and Homewood, but it was special because even then the Army made it clear that they wanted high school boys and college boys and they wanted to make a special unit of us and maybe send some of us to officers' school. So, the ministers got involved and the school officials got involved and the word was spread about this special unit. Me and my gang at Sutton's talked about nothing else until late one night we all hoisted our beers, swore a blood-oath to each other, and then waited for morning so that we could troop together down to the Army office and enlist. Even in the cool light of day, with half of us hungover enough to have second thoughts about living life itself, we went downtown and filled out the papers.

Afterwards, I wobbled to work then home to my mother to break the news. She was none too happy, but I think she knew this was going to happen, and said she understood.

I was in the second contingent of Pittsburgh boys sent to Camp Lee. There were about five hundred of us all told, and some of us couldn't help talking about how in joining the Army we were being sent back to Virginia, the very place our folks had schemed so hard to escape from. We got down there to Petersburg—that's where Camp Lee was—in early October, 1917, and it was hot, hot, like July up north. They were still constructing barracks for us, so we ended up living in tents. When we saw the barracks they were working on, we were glad we were in tents, 'cause the barracks were so crude they didn't even have windows. Of course, our living conditions were a breeze compared to our working conditions: we got down there, and believe you me, they handed every one of us jack son spade a pick a shovel a mop and told us we were now members of the 504th and 505th Service Battalions and that we were to get used to cleaning up fifty-odd acres by *every* dawn.

At first, we thought this was just our initiation into the Army: they were just trying to break us down before building us up, maybe especially because we were colored and from the North. But then after a while of this chain-gang-style nonsense, a redneck officer came by and spelled out the reality of the situation to us. He told us, gleefully almost, that we were assigned to service battalions period, no discussion. That we were never to carry arms, never to get closer than a mile to the front, that our officers were all going to be white, and that there *might* be a possibility that a very good soldier might make private first class.

Some of us heard this and thought that maybe the officer was just trying to break us down some more. But the rest heard loud and clear that no colored boy, at least at Virginia's

Camp Lee, was going to be trained for any part of a modern Army. I remember that as we argued back and forth, yelling at each other but really at the situation, someone pointed at Austin Norris and said, "Let me ask you nice, polite, go-along-with-the-program Negroes something: Norris over there just finished Yale Law School; how many of his white Yale classmates do you think are buck privates in a pick-and-shovel unit? Maybe Norris can tell us! C'mon, Norris, tell us!"

Poor Norris had nothing to say, and of course nobody else did either. After that, we took a vote and found that to a man we all wanted to be transferred to a combat unit. The trick, of course, was how to make that happen.

I don't know what a bunch of colored soldiers would do today, but then all we could think of was writing home—not to our folks, but to the ministers and school principals and to Mr. Vann at the Pittsburgh *Courier*. They had asked us to go off and make colored Pittsburgh proud; we figured they'd be hot to know we were only digging ditches. We thought maybe Mr. Vann's newspaper could expose what was happening and stir things up.

Let me tell you how the letters got written—it's sorta humorous. The fellas writing the letters took to some serious card-playing. They had a piece of beaverboard and they balanced it on their knees and, you know, played cards. But when the "coast was clear," they pocketed the cards and whipped out their writing paper and got the letters done. Austin Norris, the Yale boy, supervised this operation and saw to it that everything was done by October 31st, Halloween. Then Norris and another guy, Ode Hall, slipped off from Camp to mail the letters from Petersburg.

Norris and Hall were only supposed to be gone overnight.

When they didn't get back on time, we started to get pretty damn scared. What if the MPs caught them? What if some white man at the Petersburg post office got suspicious about seeing two colored soldiers in the lobby mailing a stack of letters to Pittsburgh, and started making phone calls? What if the letters got opened? When Norris and Hall left, we were cracking jokes about it being Halloween and there being *at least two* spooks moseying around in the moonlight. But when they didn't get back, hell, we were scared.

After two nights away, Norris and Hall slipped back into camp, as smoothly as they had gone. They had met a colored doctor in Petersburg who put them up and helped get the letters off. What's more, he had let them make some telephone calls. So, their mission had gone better than we hoped, and we knew because of the telephone calls that people in Pittsburgh already knew what we were going through at Camp Lee.

I can't tell you how tense things were while we waited to see what would happen. I'd be shoveling or disinfecting a toilet and see an MP stomping my way, and I was sure I was going to the guardhouse. A tree-size sergeant would bust in on us, and I was certain that the first words out of his mouth would be, "I hear you niggers been writing letters to Pittsburgh. . . ." We got downright paranoid when our ringleader, Norris, and another man—not Hall but Robinson—got sent off to another section of the camp and assigned to Depot Brigade. Maybe the Army was in for the slow kill, we thought: first Norris then the rest of us, not swiftly and mercifully as if by machine gun, but slowly, as if by bayonet or scalpel.

Ten days into November, Rev. Shelton Hale Bishop of Homewood's Holy Cross Episcopal Church arrived from Pittsburgh to investigate our situation firsthand. He talked with groups of men, with the commanding officers, and then with us men again. He came to see us because the Pittsburgh men whom we had called and written had met and formed a committee, and had agreed that he would be the most effective investigator. But he also came because he had boys at Camp Lee, parishioners whom he had coaxed to leave to go and fight "Bill Kaiser." Other ministers might have made the same impression on me—others probably had more boys from their churches at Camp Lee than he did. But he was the one who came, inside of ten days, and it was he whom I saw take his church members aside, 'round back our barracks, and lead them in a short service of evening prayer and communion.

I must admit that when we were doing the letterwriting and the Holy Cross boys had urged that a letter be sent to Rev. Bishop, I had joined in the teasing of them as goody goody altar boys. But that evening prayer scene, with everyone at one point even kneeling in the mud, kept coming back to me later on. Maybe Rev. Bishop, not anybody else, not even Grace, led me to the Episcopal Church once I was in Chicago.

Just before Rev. Bishop left, he told us the only thing he could promise would be that he would report that the conditions at Camp Lee were just as we had described them in the letters. He told us we were in the Army now and to take heart and be men; said he'd make his report but that we'd have to face the possibility that nothing might come of it. Let me tell you, that was one day I found out that the blues ain't just about Saturday night and your woman out the door!

One week later, fifteen of us were transferred to Camp Meade and assigned to the 351st Field Artillery. I was among the lucky fifteen. We wanted to jump and shout and throw our picks and shovels up into the bushes but we couldn't, really:

only fifteen of us were moving out to a combat unit, at least at the beginning, and lots of boys were mighty suspicious about how eight of the fifteen transfers just happened to be the men who wrote the letters to Pittsburgh. Maybe this was the Army getting back at us: agree to something and divide and conquer in the process. Of course, the Army said they weren't paying attention to names and were just moving men "mechanically," but nobody really believed that. What we did believe was that Rev. Bishop and Mr. Vann and the rest in Pittsburgh had somehow rattled some cages. As we left Camp Lee, the Camp Commander more or less said as much. No: what he *said* was we were lucky sons of bitches because most of the time a case *beginning* with "outside influences" *ended* with court martials! Lordy, that man barked and bow-wow-wowed right up to the end! But what the hell, I was off to Camp Meade, and so were one or two of my hometown partners, including Jim Haney.

"So, what about Camp Meade?" I asked my grandfather. Robert L. Stepto—Pa Step to me—crossed his legs, put his pipe down, and started in again:

Camp Meade. Well, we were happy to get there and start our artillery training. Happy? Hey, we were beside ourselves with happiness and determined to make good. But we got there and we were angry, too. For you see, we got there and discovered that the colored men already there assigned to artillery were some eighteen hundred Maryland boys from the Eastern Shore, all of them as illiterate as my dog back home. Naturally, the officers at Camp Meade were going around saying you can't train colored soldiers to be artillery men. They said that coloreds won't read the manuals or calculate the proper pitch of the gun and so forth, all the while ignoring the fact that the soldiers they were trying to train couldn't read or figure in the first place.

We got to Camp Meade, read the damn book, did the basic math to shoot the gun right, hit the damn target, and got ready for more. To their credit, the officers were pleased and they commended a bunch of us for promotions. That's when I made Corporal. We should have been pleased, I guess, but we were still angry. Hell, it was obvious: for weeks on end the Army had tried to make janitors out of educated colored men, while at the same time it had "tried" to make artillery men out of colored illiterates. Now, the white officers were all of a sudden delighted to be turning out a first-rate artillery unit of colored men, competitive with any artillery unit. Now, of course, those officers were dreaming of the promotions they'd soon have. Now, they were conveniently forgetting how much of everybody's time they had wasted proving that the Maryland colored boys sent to them couldn't do the job. Hell, some of them officers got their daily jollies proving that. We saw all that, and while we knew we were advancing and *finally* being prepared for combat, we saw all the rest.

Of course, it was also while I was at Camp Meade that I met Grace, your grandmother. I shouldn't leave that out! We got to Camp Meade in November and Thanksgiving rolled around in no time. The colored YMCA—or was it the colored WCCS?—anyway, one of them in Baltimore sent word to the camp that they were serving a Thanksgiving dinner with all the trimmings and that they'd take the first hundred boys from Meade that signed up. Me and Banks and Haney made sure we were on the list. We wanted to shake the camp dust from our feet and see Baltimore; shoot, we hadn't been in a real city if you know what I mean since leaving Pittsburgh.

Besides, and I won't lie to you, we were hoping to meet some young ladies.

"Wait a minute," I interjected. "Are you telling me that you met Grace, Ma Step I mean, at a Thanksgiving Day dinner in Baltimore?" "No, I didn't say that," he replied, grabbing up his pipe again. "What I'm telling you," he said, while sighting down his pipe at me as if it were an artillery piece, "is that there were these socials in Baltimore and that we got to going to them and that I met Grace at one of them." "Which one?" I asked. "Are you going to let me tell you, or are you going to ask fool questions?" His tone was stern, yet his eyes—his crazy, where-did-they-come-from light eyes—were smiling. "You're my grandson but shut up," was what his whole face told me, and I got quiet quick.

That Thanksgiving dinner was wonderful, and me and my gang knew we'd be heading back up to Baltimore just as soon as those nice folks invited us again. In a week or so, another announcement came, this time for a holiday social the week-end before Christmas. When we heard about that, we made double-sure we got signed up to go, 'cause you know at the Thanksgiving affair we had met some ladies and had prom-ised to see them for sure at the next social. Banks; I remem-ber Banks, good-looking and he knew it, whispering to *five* different women something like, "When I see you next, the first dance is *mine*, darling." Oh, he was out of his mind—we all were, after three months in the Army. So, what I'm telling you is that we went to that Christmas social up to Baltimore and that's where I met Grace.

When I got there, I caught up with some of my comrades already making time with the women they'd met before—or thought they'd met. I was looking for a young lady I'd had coffee with after the Thanksgiving dinner, but the woman I saw and couldn't take my eyes off of was Grace. She had a real pretty dress on and was helping with the refreshments. Everytime she handed somebody a plate of fruitcake or a cup of punch she'd look up from what she was doing and flash this wonderful, wonderful smile. I don't know . . . I was socializing with some nice people, including my best Army buddies, nobody was boring me or anything, but I just wasn't there. Somebody would speak to me and I would start to listening, but then over their shoulder, say, I'd see Grace in that pretty dress, serving cake and smiling that smile, asking even some of the most unhousebroken rascals I ever met in the Army, "Can I help you to something?"

What can I say? I guess I wanted to hear that sweet girl say, "Can I help you to something?" to me. So, I left my little crowd and went over to the refreshment table. I waited my turn for "Can I help you to something?" and got some cake. Then I got in line again, one, two, couple times more. Even though this big long table lay between us, always between us, I felt I was finally inching closer when she looked up and laughed and said, "You back again??" I asked her, "Can you take a break from serving? May I ask you to dance?" With a nod, she gestured toward the people around the other refreshment table, and said, "I'll have to ask my aunt."

"Aunt!" I said to myself. I guess I'd been out on the streets too long 'cause never once did it occur to me anymore that I'd have to get somebody's permission to dance with a girl. When I was brushing off my uniform and daydreaming about that social, that was the last thing on my mind! But there I was, walking with Grace toward her aunt before I knew it. My ears started to get redder and redder 'cause I knew I was going along with some siditty foolishness and that the boys were going to tease me all the way back to camp. But I kept walking.

We danced a couple of times and it was lovely. We talked and got to know each other a little. We talked about Chicago—even right then when we first met we talked about Chicago. She had people there, family, and liked to visit. I joked about how she just might see me there, and about how when I got there she owed me a date! As I escorted her back to her post at the refreshment table, I asked her to save the last dance of the evening for me.

Dancing with Grace as the clock stroked midnight, with that aunt of hers hawking us and all, was the tamest end to an evening I'd had in a long time. We were just about the only couple that hadn't ducked into the shadows. Still, I liked it, I liked it; I liked her. On the bus back to camp, a fella named Frank (I sort of knew him from the neighborhood back home) started razzing me: "Bet the *only* thing you got tonight was that girl's address!" Everybody started guffawing, and I chuckled, too. Frank was right, sort of—I got her address. And that was OK; that was all right. And that's how I met your grandmother.

Pa Step turned about in his chair, searching for and finding his pipe. Deftly, he cleaned it, refilled it, and settled back to enjoy himself. The pipe was a meerschaum, identical to the one he gave me for my eighteenth birthday, horrifying everyone, except me. After launching a wreath or two of smoke, he pointed the pipe at me again, and starting looking right at me, intently.

"That's how I met your grandmother," he repeated, fondling the words. I was itching to ask him a question but I couldn't. For starters, I was still smarting from being chastised for asking "fool questions" before. But he knew I wanted to ask something. Seeing me twitching in my chair, acting like I wasn't quite satisfied with his story yet, told him that. So he said, in a gentle tone that led me to open up, "You look like you're curious about something."

"Well, I am wondering . . ." I drifted. "Wondering what?" he asked, still with invitation in his voice. "Well," I began, "I always thought that you and Ma Step met on a train?" "Really," he said. An odd silence followed. For an interminable moment, the only sounds to be heard came from my fidgetings in my chair.

Clearing his throat, Pa Step asked, "And how did that story go?" "I don't know," I said, and that was the odd truth of the matter. Like many families that did not gather together, and that remembered its few reunions more for the wounds opened than for those healed, the Steptos were not storytellers. The story about Robert and Grace and the train had never been a story passed down, but rather an idle remark, thrown out over the telephone. But I had been listening, listening for something, anything. When the remark—the little snapshot—came, I had grabbed on to it; I grabbed on to it just like I had once grabbed on to a branch hanging over a fast river to keep from being thrown further downstream. But it wasn't a story yet, and after yet another round with whomever I was talking to, I knew if there was going to be a story I would have to "find" it. So, what was the story . . . ?

I was daydreaming like this when Pa Step broke in. "You don't know the story?" he asked. "You must be remembering something." "All I remember is that you and Ma Step met on a train," I began, "and that when you two ran off and got married, Aunt Grace was furious. And she told Ma Step she couldn't believe that a niece of hers had married somebody she'd met on a train that nobody knew." When I finished I was trembling. We had never before talked like we were talking now.

"Ah, that story," murmured Pa Step. He then leaned forward; both hands were tightening around his knees. "And who told you that tale?" he said. It was the old sergeant (he had made sergeant in France) who was talking to me now. In reply, I almost said again, "I don't know," which was *again* true since a dozen people had said wounding things about Pa Step in the years after Grace died. "Poor child died of a broken heart," they said; "Right in the middle of downtown," they said; and they said plenty more. So, I could have said "I don't know" and justified that because everybody was harping and it all swam together for me. But right then, the old soldier was bringing out the combatant in me, and I found myself rearing up toward him, saying, "Well, I'll tell you this: it wasn't my father!"

Pa Step smirked; he almost laughed. I was making a little scene, sounding a little righteous, but he knew even better than I did that my father needed no defense, that spreading that kind of tale was not his style. No, this was vintage venom from the womanside of the family. But who? Who might have told his grandson such a thing? Might it have been his daughter? Could it have been a daughter-in-law? They always had taken Grace's side on everything! Jesus! Could it have been Grace? Had this been one of her ways of getting even after she found out about his affairs?

The smirk long gone, Pa Step sat still in his chair, clouded up and brooding. He fingered his pipe, looked at me, glanced out the window, then snapped around and glared at me hard. When he spoke he hissed, "The only train I was on with your grandmother was the train to Chicago the day after we married. Yes, I came on to her, but we were married. And I had a right!"

Missouri Weather

Margaret Hartshorn lived forty years as a slave and fifty years as a freewoman, and had a way of talking about slavery that made it sound a bit better than freedom. She had been a slave in northern Virginia, probably in Fairfax County, and she was probably a slave of the Hartshorn who ran a toll road in Alexandria and who was once in business with George Washington—"probably" because the other Hartshorn in the neighborhood was a Quaker. In slavery, Margaret was a house servant, and her husband, Louis Hartshorn, may have been one as well, though he later proved to be a capable farmer. They had their children in those days; the first child born after freedom was a grandchild.

Margaret was a fabulous storyteller. When she regaled her grandchildren, and later her great-grandchildren, with her stories, the stories were about slavery times and what she called her "privileges." One story she told was about the time mistress reprimanded her for disciplining her own child. "I got so mad at mistress I picked her up and put her in the fireplace!" Margaret would declare. "Mistress jumped out of that fireplace and started wagging her bony finger at me, saying all the while, 'I'm going to tell master this time! Gonna tell master!'" Margaret would be chuckling at this point. "And she told master when he got home, and you know what he did? He *came* after me and kinda *cornered* me in the kitchen, and said, 'Margaret, please don't do that again!' That's right! That's what happened: 'Margaret, *please* don't do that!'" Everybody laughed.

Another kind of story was the "goin' to town" story. Town was Washington, D.C., and every monument and every building of consequence that was erected in the District from the 1820s to 1860 was observed by Margaret, with almost an architect's eye for detail. She had a story about the Washington Monument, and another about the White House, but her favorite inspiration was the Smithsonian Institution. She was thirty years old when that Romanesque concoction was begun, and every tower, every belfry, fascinated her endlessly. She was still storytelling about the Smithsonian when her great-grandchildren came along. One of them later told of going off to Washington to college at Howard and recognizing the Smithsonian building immediately—Margaret's descriptions of it had been just that vivid and accurate.

But the great story of slavery had been one of freedom as well. It was the story of how Louis had bought his freedom and then purchased Margaret's. Louis, or maybe he and Margaret together, must have struck a bargain for their children, too, for when they left Virginia for northwest Missouri in 1860, they had children in tow.

This story was a source of great pride and hence the crown jewel of Margaret's stories, but it was also the last one in her story-hoard. Once Margaret got to this one, she didn't carry forward with tales of Missouri and the adventures of freedom, she backed up: Virginia and the District and the castles of the Smithsonian always were more appealing to her than the dull sights and leaden twangs of Missouri, even though Virginia was about slavery and Missouri, at least for her and hers, was not. Margaret had no stories about Missouri; this was her way of saying she'd rather sing of old slavery times than sing the blues.

Margaret and Louis got out to Missouri in 1860, and while they found a good piece of land, they found everything else disheartening. The area they moved to was distinctly western and full of the westward ho! spirit, even though the time when fifteen hundred wagons a year would cross the Missouri River at St. Joseph to venture into the plains was mostly over. Yet the area was also distinctly southern and redneck: full of the flotsam and jetsam that floated over from Kentucky and Tennessee, and that washed up from Arkansas, looking for that mythical America in which common white men could be kings. The Hartshorns found themselves in Mark Twain's Missouri, only their white neighbors were the Twainian characters who had rousted themselves, and who had left the sleepy Mississippi riverbank towns to try once again at prosperity on the banks of the Missouri.

So, the Hartshorns found themselves both west and south: west enough to have land and live on it, south enough to be constantly reminded—certainly by the two thousand slaves in their midst—that they were Negroes living in the United States, and succeeding only by the grace of God and by the whims of the peculiar Missouri weathers, political and otherwise.

In 1860, Margaret and Louis didn't dare try to vote in the Presidential election—they weren't ready for that. But they did care about the returns, knowing that that would tell them something about where they had come to live. The results were discouraging: Abe Lincoln came in dead last in the county, with only 452 votes, 410 of those coming from city folk in St. Joseph. Out in the country where they were, only forty two people had had the conviction to vote for Lincoln. Louis was concerned, but he said to Margaret, "Least there are some people out here who think our way." Margaret wasn't so sure; she started worrying about her children, fretting about crossing over the Missouri into Kansas.

Then the War came, and the Hartshorns got another big picture of the Missouri they had moved to. While 110,000 Missouri men joined the Union forces (including 8,000 Negroes), 40,000 other Missouri men went off to join the Confederacy, including almost 2,000 from their county. The Hartshorns were in town, in St. Joseph, that day in 1861 when the white folks got to fighting over whether the Federal flag should fly above the post office. Louis surveyed the scene, and with unheard of composure said to Margaret, "Darling. I thinks we best be gettin' home." She for once had no rejoinder; she just nodded her head and sprang up into the wagon before Louis had even taken a step.

Louis got the farm going nicely, partly because the children were big enough to help, but he still didn't much like Missouri, especially when he compared it to Virginia. He was known to say, "I'd rather go out in the woods and talk to the trees than bother with the people 'round here." Margaret had her own way of putting it. She declared, "Missouri ain't nothing but hogs and hominy." Unfortunately, neither Louis nor

Margaret ever tired of these ventilations. They went on this way for years, decades. Even with their grandchildren, the first thing they said to them when they came into this world was, "Sorry you had to be born here."

The lion's share of these grumblings were pummeled upon the first grandchild, Margaret "Maggie" Hawkins, who was singled out for being pitifully the first in the family born away from Virginia. The situation only became worse for Maggie as she grew up, especially after her parents died and she and her brother, Will, went to live with the Hartshorns. After three excruciating years, Maggie married young, at seventeen; that was the first thing she did to get some distance from her grandparents.

Then she started to get even: when she had her children, she made a point of not naming any of the three boys after Louis, or any of the four girls after Margaret. Not naming a girl after Margaret was its own special statement. There had always been a Margaret: Maggie was a Margaret, her mother was a Margaret, and of course, glaring down on the generations from the pinnacle of her matriarchy was Margaret Hartshorn. But Maggie put an end to it. No one knew exactly what Maggie was saying by doing this, but clearly she was making her own break from the past.

Maggie's husband, eight years her senior, was a "bright mulatto" from Kentucky named Joseph Smith Burns. Everybody knew Smith, as he was called, had had a white father named Floyd; what they didn't know was whether Floyd was a first name or a last name. Smith Burns was a good farmer, maybe the best of the colored farmers. Louis Hartshorn gave Smith and Maggie some land when they married; Smith made those acres sing with productivity. Soon, in 1880, Smith and Maggie started producing children, too.

Margaret Hartshorn probably told her great-grand-children, as she had told her grandchildren, how sorry she was that they had had to be born in Missouri. She doubtless, too, had commiserations for Smith Burns's Kentucky roots, and chidings for Maggie for not at least *trying* to find a hus-band from Virginia. Maybe Margaret meant only to tease, but Maggie and Smith did not hear her that way. Margaret should have had a little foresight: if she had held her tongue, things might have gone better between them all when Louis died and she was forced to move in with Maggie and Smith.

In 1888, the city of St. Joseph built the county's first col-ored high school. When the first graduation ceremony oc-curred, colored folk from far and near, including Maggie and Smith, showed up for the event. Afterward, Maggie was deter-mined to see her children attend the high school, even if it meant giving up the farm. Smith did not want to give up the farm—he was a good farmer. Maggie kept up her campaign, though; she poked and she prodded, she hinted and she whee-dled, she put her foot down (several times) and got what she wanted.

By the mid-1890s, the Burns family was living in St. Jo-seph, and the Burns children were starting to attend the high school. Smith Burns found himself in a city house on a city street surrounded by Maggie, children, his brother-in-law, Will (Maggie's brother), and Margaret Hartshorn. He would put up with that for ten years.

Margaret Hartshorn lived through slavery and freedom, through much of the building of the nation's capitol and through the Civil War. She was already elderly when, in St. Joseph, the Pony Express was formed, when Jesse James was betrayed and shot dead, and when the colored people finally got a high school. She lived to see the new century and with it the first graduations of her people from high school and college. She also lived long enough to see a granddaughter make sure that there would be no more girls named Margaret, at least for a while.

Smith Burns was fifty-five years old in 1900, and he found himself living in St. Joseph, a city of 100,000 people, not where he was supposed to be—on his farm. Granted, his wife was happy and his children were attending far better schools than there were in the country; two had already finished high school. But the garden patch out back the house was not acres of good field, and the backroom jobs he found at a local department store would never satisfy the wants and needs of a born farmer.

His house was good enough, big by the standards of the day—selling the farm he had hated to sell had brought in enough money for a decent house in town. But living there was claustrophobic, suffocating. The first son, Arthur, was gone; though smart enough to be valedictorian at the high school, he had also proved dumb enough to be lured into the fast life in Chicago. Second son, Randolph—"Dolph" amongst his people—was teaching school, and had his own little place now. But that still left four children at home, starting with Ocie at fourteen and ending with Ina Belle at one. Then there was Will, his brother-in-law, twenty-eight years old and living with them, still trying to find his way. And there was Margaret Hartshorn, Mother Hartshorn as they had taken to calling her; ramrod straight, Bible-thumping, still talking about Virginia like she had been of one of the first families. She was under their roof for the duration. And of course there was Maggie, his wife; not a big woman, but Lord! she took up a lot of space; filled it with her plans, her pronouncements, her opinions.

So, Smith Burns was looking for some space, some breathing room, and where he found it, not having any land anymore, was at church. All looked good for a time: Maggie and Mother Hartshorn went around crowing that they had not only brought Smith Burns to the city, but to God as well. But neither woman was so consumed in her religiosity that she failed to notice that what Smith Burns was getting at church, besides power, was the attentions of women, plenty of women. Out in the country, on the farm, Smith Burns had been just another farmer. But in town, in the city, he was a light skinned man with blow hair and a downtown job, however modest it was. He looked good to women. Maggie got worried, and Mother Hartshorn oddly was of no help: all she could manage was to tell tale after tale about how back in Virginia there was always some "mulatto-type Negro" fomenting commotion, when all anybody wanted to do was live in peace.

Smith Burns looked for his moment, not to run away with one of the ladies, but just to get away. He pinned his hopes on his boys and on their returning to St. Joseph to take care of things. Arthur soon made it clear that he was gone for good, through with St. Joseph, through with school and uplift. He was in Chicago, and about to become the headwaiter at the TipTop Club. Dolph on the other hand had returned and was teaching school. Then word came that Ocie was finishing the work he had found in Egypt after Tuskegee, and he was coming home as well. Smith Burns thought hard: if Dolph is here, if Ocie is here, I can break away.

In 1905, Smith Burns left his family and Missouri for what Colorado promised him, but his departure wasn't exactly to plan. He had counted on Ocie's return, and Ocie had returned, but what he hadn't counted on was Dolph having the gumption to announce that he wasn't going to teach in St. Joseph's colored schools the rest of his life, and that he was going off to Howard Medical School. So it was young Ocie, not the established and salaried Dolph, who came to head the family. Then Dolph returned from medical school, not to help out, but to die. What was left of the family buried Dolph in 1906 out at Mt. Mora Cemetery. Later, when Arthur died, the two of them shared a double-sided tombstone.

The family story has it that when Smith Burns "lit out for the territory" he left behind both his family *and* his race. This may be true, and like most "passing" stories it certainly offers a reason for Smith's never returning. But it also may be a fantasy willingly told because it is easier to accuse Smith of passing than to face and accept how miserable he was while living with your kin—maybe with you. Also, and oddly enough, to say Smith passed is to caress his face; it is to admire his carriage, it is to declare all over again that, wrong as he was to leave the family, he sure was pretty.

Smith Burns did not return for Dolph's funeral in 1906; certainly not for Margaret Hartshorn's in 1907. He did not appear for Ocie's wedding in December of 1907—an occasion that lifted the hearts of many after so much death and woe. His youngest daughter, Inabel, offered in 1977 this one memory of him: he let me play with his hair. He would sit in the kitchen reading his newspaper, and he would let me braid and braid his hair. By her account, that would have been in 1903 or '04. By 1905, he was gone.

Will Hawkins (William Daniel Hawkins) was only five or six when death took away both of his parents. So, when he and his older sister, Maggie, went to live with their grandparents, the Hartshorns, he didn't have the same stock of memories Maggie had of their parents—there just hadn't been enough time to accumulate them. In a sense, this made it easier for the Hartshorns to raise him, for unlike the petulant, adolescent Maggie, Will had little basis for sucking his teeth and saying things like, "Poppa taught me different" or "Momma never made me do that." Under the Hartshorn regimen, Maggie raged but Will thrived.

The Hartshorns raised Will to be a good, God-fearing boy, but they did not douse all his fires. In high school, Will had a sweetheart, and despite all the Bible-thumping and all the strictures of colored high Victorianism, Will and his sweetheart became lovers. Of course, they still went to church and to the church socials; they had proper parlor visits, and they made a show of timidly holding hands. But they had a passion, an appetite for each other. The only evidence of caution they offered was that Mildred (that was her name) didn't get pregnant until *after* they graduated from high school.

In May of 1892, just before his twentieth birthday, Will became a father. There was no pussyfooting around on the question of paternity: the boy was Will's boy, and he was proudly named William Daniel Hawkins, Jr. Why Will and Mildred didn't get married remains a mystery; surely there were people in both families who felt that only a wedding could absolve the disgrace. But there was no wedding, and Will went on living with his sister Maggie and with Mother Hartshorn, even when he knew that he was part of the crowding problem in the Burns house.

Mildred and baby William remained in St. Joseph for years—perhaps in the beginning Mildred thought there might still be a marriage—then they took off for Colorado, which seemed the promised land for every colored person not set on going to Chicago. Will stayed in St. Joe and married Cordelia Coleman, a twenty-seven-year-old schoolteacher who also played the piano and organ for weddings and church services. At the age of twenty-eight, Will had finally landed on his feet.

Something to be puzzled out about Will is his history of being taken in, as if life for him was always a search for that threshold or hearth promising a sheltering embrace. The Hartshorns took him in when he was a boy; that started the pattern. Sister Maggie took him in along with Mother Hartshorn when he was young man; he'd stay with her until he was almost thirty. The affair with Mildred possibly began with a version of her taking him in; perhaps it ended, too, precisely because Will wasn't looking to create a family—he was still moving *into* families. Then came Cordelia and the Colemans: 1713 Angelique Street became Will's address, but it had already been the Coleman address for more than twenty years; of their taking Will in there can be no doubt.

The most extraordinary expression of this came when Thomas and Louise Coleman, Cordelia's parents, helped the young couple "find" their own house. This took the form of Thomas building them a house with his own hands, just as he had built his own house. The new house went up on the same lot with the existing Coleman house, side-by-side with it. It was identical to the older house in every outward detail, as if the first house had suddenly found its long lost twin. While there were soon two houses, the second house did not acquire its own address. The address for both was 1713 Angelique Street. The Colemans had married off their "spinster" daughter without casting her out; Will Hawkins had finally found a marriage, and a house of his own, while still avoiding being on his own. Indeed, he had moved in again with somebody. This would be the arrangement for the thirty years left in his life.

Will and Cordelia lost their first baby, a girl, but successfully brought forth a boy in November of 1904: Coleman Randolph Hawkins. Why "Randolph" was chosen as a name is open to question; perhaps they were honoring the young but already beloved "Dolph" Burns, Will's nephew, who had already become principal of one of the colored schools. But "Coleman" as the boy's first name is an easy read. Granted these people were southerners, and as partial as were their white counterparts to the southern tradition of bestowing a mother's maiden name as a child's given name. But more was afoot. Think again of those two twin houses: a Coleman house and a Hawkins house in one glance; two Coleman houses, built by the same Coleman, in another view. That child had to be named Coleman; one is almost surprised that the boy wasn't named Coleman Coleman Hawkins!

From the beginning, Coleman Hawkins was a Coleman family project. Cordelia was adept on the piano and the organ; her father, Thomas, perhaps because he was the sexton at Christ Episcopal Church, had had the opportunity to learn the organ as well. Will loved music, too, but lagged behind his wife and father-in-law in his skills. (Coleman would later say, not unkindly, that his father encouraged him in music as much as his mother did, but that his father could only play one tune, something he had made up.) There was no question in the family about raising Coleman to be a musician, though they were not thinking of it being his livelihood. The project was to make a thorough gentleman of him, to be certain that he would be a man of several gifts of which music would be one, just as another man might have the gift of French or Italian.

Will Hawkins watched while his son learned to read music before he learned to read; he noted how his son was drawn to the piano all the while Cordelia was foisting a cello upon him, and paying "Professor" Pennell for expensive cello lessons. Trouble came when Cordelia determined that Coleman was shirking his cello practice; after that, she marched him out to the shed in the backyard where he could practice without distractions. Nobody called that "woodshedding" then, but clearly with the cello, and later with the saxophone, Coleman was "woodshedding" before he was ten years old.

Given that the Burnses and the Hawkinses and related families had radically changed their lives in the 1890s so that their children could attend the colored high school in St. Joseph, it is amazing that when Will and Cordelia's boy came of high school age they sent him off to Topeka to an Institute that was a sort of Tuskegee of the plains. Will probably would have been glad to see Coleman stay home; without doubt, he would have preferred not to see Cordelia take a job as matron of the downtown Ladies' restroom just so Coleman's tuition could be paid. But again, Cordelia had an agenda: the Institute promised both an education and a certain environment. Cordelia expressed what she hoped that environment would be like when she made Coleman take his cello with him—and leave his saxophone behind.

Coleman made a few trips home from Topeka, but basically he was gone, gone for the rest of life. Certainly after 1922, when Cordelia relented and let Coleman join Mamie Smith's band, he was to be forever on the road and frequently out of touch. Coleman's departure was but one weighing heavily upon Will: Ocie Burns, who had returned in 1905 to head the Burns family, had moved with his wife and children to Chicago; Maggie, Will's sister, had decided to live with her youngest daughter in Kansas City; and Thomas Coleman, the true patriarch of 1713 Angelique Street, had just passed away. That meant that Will was all of sudden living with just Cordelia and her mother, with virtually no kin around the corner or down the street. Who was going to take him in?

On March 4th of 1935 (by some accounts, March 5th), about a year after Coleman settled in Europe, Will Hawkins took his life. He did so not with pills, or with a leap from a building; he did not jump in front of a train or a truck. He walked down Francis Street to the Missouri River, and when he got to the river, he kept going, deeper and deeper into the waters, until he was cold and numb and overtaken, and swept away. It took two months to find Will's body; when it was discovered it was found on the Kansas banks, near Atchison. He made it to the other shore.

Two accounts of Will's suicide appeared in the newspapers, one a front-page story, the other an obituary. They share much of the same language, and could well have been written by the same reporter. Both pieces begin by marveling at how "nonchalant" Will was, as he stood on the banks of the Missouri at Francis Street and "lighted his pipe, adjusted his glasses, buttoned his overcoat, and walked to his death." However, while the obituary refers to Will as William, the front-page story calls him Bill. The front page also inserts "colored," as in "Bill Hawkins, colored." This perhaps makes his nonchalance all the more extraordinary.

The second paragraph of the front-page story seductively deepens the mystery and incites curiosity: "Miss Cornelius Plato and Arthur Adams, employees of the Pioneer Sand Co, saw Hawkins in the water and said that he floated in an eddy several minutes before he disappeared. Andrew Schleicher, another witness, said that Hawkins looked at a yellow piece of paper before he walked into the water." What was on the yellow piece of paper? The obituary in contrast seeks witnesses who knew of his despondency yet hastened to add "to know him would efface from your mind the least thought that such would be the end of the life of one whom many had learned to esteem."

The gentler obituary continues in its review of where Will worked, concluding "he established a record of efficient and dependable service that was a credit not only to himself, but to his race." In its where-did-Will-work paragraph, the front-page story simply identifies the business, American Electric, and reports neither Will's efficiency nor his dependability but rather his absence from work that morning.

The front-page story ends there; the obituary necessarily goes on to list of Will's survivors. Again, one notices how so many people related to Will are living elsewhere, flung to where fortune and hope have taken them: Colorado, Chicago, St. Louis, Europe. To read that list is give the term "distant relative" new meaning. Indeed, Coleman, Will's son, did not even hear of the death until a year later. He hadn't been in touch for two years and no one knew how to reach him. With the help of *Downbeat* magazine and a Swiss jazz reporter named Ernest Berner, Cordelia finally got a letter to Coleman, informing him of what Will had done. There is no record of Coleman's reply.

Will Hawkins was buried in May of 1935 in a section of Mt. Mora Cemetery known as the Northwest Privilege, where Louise Coleman had bought a series of plots when her husband Thomas died. Will was buried adjacent to Thomas. Later, when Louise and finally Cordelia died (both women living to be almost one hundred), they were nestled into the ground next to Thomas and Will. When a stone went up it was a handsome stone, no expense spared. But it was again, in keeping with the strange family custom, a double-sided stone: memorials for Thomas and Louise Coleman expressed on one side, sentiments for William and Cordelia Hawkins offered on the other. Will Hawkins sought in marrying Cordelia Coleman a family that would take him in, and the Colemans took him in for eternity. Even now, they share one address.

Ina Belle Burns was the seventh and last child born to Maggie and Smith Burns. Arriving as she did when Maggie was almost forty, Ina may have been a "love child," conceived in the hope that its presence would rekindle a failing marriage. If so, it didn't work; Smith was out the door a few years later.

Ina was born with an eye condition and was legally blind until she was eight or nine, when the condition improved. That meant that she had to be tended to, not just when she was very young but older. Maggie couldn't do it; after Smith left, she had to work. So, Ina was left in the care of Mother Harts-horn, who tenderly called her her "poor 'flicted child." To-gether all day, they would sing and tell Bible stories, and Mother Hartshorn would tell her slavery stories, too. That is how her slavery stories (the only ones the family has) got passed down to the present: she told them to Ina, and Ina made a point of remembering them, passing them along to others, including me.

Ina sensed Mother Hartshorn's love, but not Maggie's. Ina considered her mother cold and aloof. This may have been true, but Maggie may also have appeared that way because she was tired, tired from her work as a domestic, and tired from running her own house, too. Two things stuck in Ina's craw regarding her mother: Maggie hadn't clipped and kept as a keepsake a lock of Ina's hair, as she had done with the other children, and Maggie hadn't named Ina Margaret. Maggie had had four daughters, and hence four opportunities to name a girl Margaret and keep the tradition going; Ina's older sis-ters seemed not to care about this, but Ina did, and fiercely. Even as a child, she was drawn to causes.

After Ina's eye condition cleared up, she finally entered the local school. Thanks to the years of tutoring by her brothers, she was placed in the fourth grade, and she did well. By the eighth grade, Ina had become a star student, especially in the writing of compositions. That year, she decided to enter the essay contest sponsored by the Tuberculosis Association. Dolph had died of tuberculous; other family members had suffered it; Ina felt she had something to say. Two prizes were awarded: first prize, which went to a white eighth grader, and the "Negro prize," which was Ina's.

Though young, Ina could see what had happened: because she was colored, the judges hadn't wanted to give her first prize, or even a share of first prize; but, out of a peculiar sense of fairness, they hadn't wanted to give her second prize, either. So, they invented a "Negro prize" and thought Ina would be delighted with it. She wasn't, and neither was anyone else in the Burns house. The family crowded around the kitchen table and talked it over. The advice they gave Ina was to keep the essay and to write another one in a year. She was to compare the two and judge for herself which one was better. Forget the contest judges, they said; learn how to judge your work on your own.

The prize episode altered Ina, forcing her to grow up in certain ways almost instantly, but it wasn't the only change for her that year. The other change was of her own invention: she changed her name—not to Margaret, as one might have expected; she had been hit hard by the death of Mother Hartshorn a few years before—but to Inabel Frances. Inabel obviously was a combining of Ina and Belle; it was also her own personal reconfiguration of a name she hated sharing with a white girl nearby (could this have been the eighth-grader who won first prize?). Frances she adopted because it had been Smith Burns's mother's name. This was how she addressed the Margaret business: if she wasn't going to be allowed the name of her maternal women, she was going to take a name from her father's line. She was determined not to be "nameless."

Inabel went off to Howard University in 1916. She had her heart set on attending Howard not just because it was a good school but because brother Dolph had attended medical school there (however briefly). Dolph struck out on his own path in going to Howard; Inabel sought that, too. Mother Hartshorn, dead for nine years now, was in her thoughts as well. In going off to Washington, Inabel knew full well that she was going back to where the family had begun, back where Louis and Margaret Hartshorn had bought their freedom fifty-six years before, back to the city that so enthralled Margaret Hartshorn with its buildings and monuments.

At Howard, Inabel was elected to certain "proper" organizations including the Stylus Club (the literary group; Zora Neale Hurston would be a member five years later) and the Alpha Kappa Alpha sorority, of which she would later be chapter president. But she also gravitated toward other, more political concerns. She founded the Women's Suffrage League unit at Howard, for example, and held nothing back when she often took the podium. At least one of her addresses must have stirred a commotion: it was entitled, "Woman, the Masterpiece of Creation."

Inabel was on the move, doing things she felt constrained from even considering back in Missouri; she was growing in hundreds of directions, some of which seemed contradictory. She joined the Episcopal Church, for example, because she detested the crowds of students heading for the other churches. "Who'd want to be part of a herd?" she'd say. At the same time, there was hardly ever a campus strike while Inabel attended Howard that didn't have her at the forefront. The "legendary" dining hall strike of 1919, led in part by Inabel (she wanted more salads!), played a role in her meeting her husband-to-be, fellow student Arnett Lindsay. He was not a comrade striker;

in fact, as headwaiter of the dining hall, he was part of management and on the other side. She was one of those rabble-rousers, but he watched her in action and was attracted. Later he explained, "She was working against me, because this was my livelihood at the time. But I couldn't help but admire her persistence and determination. . . ."

In her senior year, Inabel discovered she didn't want to work at what she was training to do: teach school. Back in St. Joseph, people had no conception of black women doing anything other than teach or nurse; that's why all her sisters were either teachers or nurses. But in Washington and at Howard, Inabel saw handfuls of women, no different or better trained than herself, challenging the barriers and reaching for the possibilities in new fields. Inabel was on their side, and indeed wanted to one of them. It wasn't just that she wanted to do something new, she wanted to be in on the *battles* that come when women do something new. Outside her family at least, she was developing a taste for friction.

But what would this new field be? Inabel's advisor, Howard's librarian, suggested social work, and she looked into it, knowing all the while that she was risking the wrath of the family. They had sent her to Howard and paid her fees; they expected her to study education and to return to St. Joe as a schoolteacher. Mother Maggie didn't just expect this, she demanded it. How was Inabel going to get around that? At her advisor's urging, she applied to social work schools anyway, and won an Urban League Fellowship to the New York School of Social Work.

Winning the fellowship was easier than facing her family. Inabel badly wanted to go to New York but knew she couldn't

BLUE AS THE LAKE

without their blessing. Maggie predictably was hostile to the idea. "I'm not going to let a daughter of mine go off to New York!" she said. She was amazed and angered that Inabel would be attracted to social work: "I can't believe you want to work with those people in the slums!"

Inabel despaired of turning Maggie around; she even prepared a letter declining the fellowship. But her sister Ola and sister-in-law Mildred Burns (Ocie's wife) told her not to send the letter before they had approached Maggie once more. A week later, Maggie relented and offered her reluctant consent. At the dawn of the Harlem Renaissance, with so many black people traveling to New York to chase their dreams, Inabel was heading to New York, too. She had won another year of independence.

She had one good year there: her classes went well; her fieldwork in Harlem and in Brooklyn taught her some lessons in the real world. Sundays, Inabel and Arnett Lindsay (he was studying business at NYU) dined at the cheap but good restaurants students discover, and then went on bus rides to see the sights. It was a good year, but only one year: letters, then telegrams, arrived with anxious messages about Maggie's declining health; Inabel knew she had to return home as soon the school year was over.

Inabel fretted about finding work back home. St. Joseph had real social problems, but there were no social agencies, and there certainly was no Urban League office. She was thinking of seeking work at the YWCA—she had worked in one in Washington—but when she arrived home, she found she had a teaching job waiting for her. At Maggie's behest, one of her sisters had taken Inabel's Howard transcript and diploma down to the board of education and had applied for a fifth-grade position for her. Maggie and the rest said they were "just trying to help," and Inabel dutifully thanked them. But she was beginning to see just how much Maggie intended for her to live the life that had been planned for her.

Inabel took the teaching job, but as soon as the school year ended, she traveled to Cleveland to work for its Urban League. She was meeting her fellowship commitment to the Urban League, but she was also seeking respite from St. Joseph and the family cocoon. In a related move, she applied for and got a teaching job in Kansas City—fifty miles from St. Joe. She needed the better pay, and she needed breathing room, too. But when she returned from Cleveland, a note was waiting for her, pinned to the front door. It read: "I've gone ahead to Kansas City and rented a house for *us*. Here's the address. Love, Mother Maggie." (The italics were Inabel's.)

The first thing Inabel did in Kansas City was to find a better house than the one Maggie had rented—a house of her *own* choosing. Then she went to the school, the toughest black elementary school in town, and met her principal and colleagues. Inabel knew she was in for it when the principal began the staff meeting by saying, "This year, we have two college graduates joining our faculty. I don't know why the board keeps hiring them and sending them here. We don't need them, and *I* don't like them."

Inabel went to her classroom and found forty ruffians, as tough, abused, and neglected as any children she had encountered in her casework in New York. Months later, she wasn't sure how much she had taught them, but she knew she had an orderly classroom; she had been teaching manners, and she had been working as a social worker would have with some of the children and their families.

Inabel got out of the Kansas City schools, and out of teaching, in 1925 by marrying Arnett Lindsay. Maggie may have been angered by Inabel leaving the schools but there was nothing she could do about it: Missouri still enforced the antique law prohibiting married women from the classroom. Inabel and Arnett settled in St. Louis, where he was in business. Arnett must have wanted Inabel very badly, because marrying her meant taking in Mother Maggie, too. He soon learned the advantage to having Maggie about: she did housework, which Inabel detested. Maggie also helped him with the cooking; they traded recipes.

Free from teaching, Inabel did not immediately return to social work, though she relished the fact that there were agencies in St. Louis where she could work. She didn't work because she had pledged to Arnett that she would stay home for a year and try to conceive a child. Arnett was a progressive man on the matter of women working, but in 1925, at the beginning of their marriage, he needed some appeasing. Perhaps Maggie did, too; perhaps to keep the peace with Maggie Inabel had to gently, not abruptly, slip back into her chosen work.

After eleven restless months, the Urban League came to her rescue, as Inabel would later put it. They asked if she would join Charles S. Johnson in conducting fieldwork in Springfield, Illinois. Arnett proved to be reasonable about this: "You got a chance to work with Dr. Johnson," he said,

"Take it!" She did. The project lasted six months, and she got a lot out of it, including her first job offers back in St. Louis.

Inabel was hired as a family caseworker for the private St. Louis Provident Association. When the Depression hit, the St. Louis Relief Administration was formed, ushering in the era of government welfare agencies. Inabel went to work for the government, starting as a senior caseworker, and worked up to be a district supervisor. There was no turning back: Inabel was a full-fledged social worker, with growing seniority. She liked going to work and she liked coming home, especially since she knew her dinner and her martini were waiting.

Maggie Burns died in 1936, struck by a stroke while walking to church. Inabel grieved, and made sure that Maggie was properly buried in the family plot back in St. Joseph. But she wasted no time in making her plans. She arranged a leave from her agency and enrolled in the University of Chicago's School of Social Work that fall. In Chicago, she would be close to Ocie and Mildred in the first months after Maggie's death, and she would finally complete the degree Maggie had prevented her from completing sixteen years before.

Toward the end of that year in Chicago, E. Franklin Frazier telephoned Inabel from Howard: he wanted her to return there and help build up its Department of Social Work. Now that she had her degree, he said, a faculty appointment was possible. Inabel wanted to try university-level teaching; she definitely wanted to return to Washington as well. She got no quarrel from Arnett: his business in St. Louis had gone sour in the Depression; he was happy for a fresh start.

Thus did Inabel return to Washington. Arnett became a successful real estate broker. Inabel helped build Howard's Department of Social Work into the School of Social Work. Inabel became its Dean, and the first woman academic dean in Howard's history. But first, she had to jump through the hoop of being *director* of the School. Moreover, in meetings with Howard's president, he called her *daughter.* "Let's hear what daughter Lindsay has to say!" My, how she must have gritted her teeth.

Inabel Burns Lindsay was a great-granddaughter of the Hartshorns, who were born in slavery. She was a daughter of Maggie and Smith Burns, who left their farm to go to town where their children could attend high school. She was a niece of Will Hawkins and hence a first cousin of jazz legend Coleman Hawkins. While other family members left Missouri for Chicago or the West, she retraced the path back to Washington and the East. In the District of Columbia, she lived among the buildings and monuments Margaret Hartshorn gawked at a century before from the back of a farm wagon. In the District now, on the Howard campus, there is a building named Inabel Burns Lindsay Hall. Margaret Hartshorn would have hated the architecture, so unlike that of the Smithsonian. But she would have smiled and smiled to see a building, in the District no less, named for her poor 'flicted child.

One of Inabel's stories about being a Depression-era social worker involved a wild-eyed man who stomped into her agency one morning. He needed gas coupons so he could use his truck on a job he'd scared up. Inabel helped him cut through the bureaucracy and get his coupons in ten minutes. He was so grateful that he started shouting, "She's an angel!

She's an angel!" Inabel thought that was amazing; we in the family did, too—Inabel was no angel.

Inabel—Aunt Inie to me—was what we now call a "piece of work," in great part because of what she was running from in Missouri and running toward in the East. While it is tempting to speak of the differences among the family women—juxtaposing, for example, Margaret Hartshorn's illiteracy with Inabel's higher degrees—the real thing to see was that they were all hard-willed, kick-ass women. They all were supervisors. Inabel stood out because she wasn't interested in domestic supervising; she wanted to run things out in public, and in the halls of agencies and academies.

To say that Inabel wasn't interested in the domestic is not to say she ignored the familial: she had advice, and she could meddle right up there in Maggie's league. She went after Marge and Anna, Ocie and Mildred's daughters, like a drill sergeant, barking for more backbone, agitated that they had "regressed" and done something as commonplace as becoming schoolteachers. When my father went to Howard Medical School, Inabel gave him no rest, cleverly explaining that her *niece* had asked her to keep an eye on him. When it was decided that I would attend private school, Inabel mounted a campaign for me to come and live with her in Washington and attend St. Albans. St. Albans didn't admit black students in those days, but that was going to be part of the fun of it for Inabel: Let's see who is going to tell me my nephew can't enroll in St. Albans! My sister did follow Inabel into social work, but there was no way she was going to train at Howard; even at Atlanta where she did enroll she worried about Inabel's phone calls to her professors.

So, you learned to approach Inabel like a cat approaches a

hot stove—gingerly. Yet, even if you did not appreciate all her quirks and passions, you had to admire the fact that she had cultivated a style. Part of her style was to come at something slantwise, or just a little off center, as in making a point of attending an Episcopal church that shared space with a synagogue. She drank, which the women in her generation in the family rarely did, and she drank scotch; in the family, who knew anyone who did that? Likewise, when she wrote out her funeral instructions, she insisted on being buried in St. Joe at Mt. Mora beside everyone else in the Northwest Privilege (never mind the fact that she hadn't been in St. Joseph for thirty years). But, typical of Inabel, she was to be cremated first, with the urn of ashes then placed in cement! Who had heard of that?

But what was most slantwise was Inabel's marriage: in Arnett, she found a husband who wanted children but would not insist upon them; a husband who would join her in the complicated task of loving and putting up with Maggie in her last years; and also, a husband who knew he was still a man after shopping for dinner and cooking it. What he got in return, most obviously, was a wife successful in her profession, who helped him with the social side of his business, and who encouraged him to be as successful as he could as an independent historian in his off-hours.

The example of their marriage, while spurned by most every couple that has come since in the family, is a fascination to me. My comfort in the kitchen, and more especially, my comfort in markets of all kinds, has something to do with Arnett, and with my going with him to the outdoor stands in Washington for the best fish, the best fruit. There seems also to be a profound connection between Inie and Arnett publishing everything they wrote after they found each other, and Michele and I doing the same. One huge difference is that we produced babies as well as books, but that is largely explained by changing times and differing pressures. If Inie and Arnett had been launching careers in the 1970s, as we did, not the 1920s, they may have had children, too.

Inabel was "slantwise" but she was also direct. In the workplace in the 1930s in Missouri, she conspicuously walked out of a major social work conference when an invited judge began his remarks with a "darkie" joke. But she was directly up front at home as well. In old age, Inabel lost a leg, due to diabetes, and was fitted with a prosthesis. We visited soon after. At one point, she asked our then ten-year-old son, Gabe, if he knew what a prosthesis was. He said no. She then yanked off her artificial leg from its stump as quickly as a samarai might draw his sword, and said, "Gabriel, this is a prosthesis!" We had been trying to find a way to explain Inie's new condition to our son; Inabel just took charge and made the explanation herself. That was how she operated.

None of the Missouri women would have handled the situation that way. Inabel was Inabel, full of her own particular weather.

Lester Leaps In

Miss Burns was sitting in her favorite parlor chair, the red one, talking on the phone with Miss York (she called her *York!* in the same tone someone else would say *Duck!* or *Stop!*) when the doorbell rang. Miss Burns ignored the bell at first—Miss York's gossip was getting just that good—then it rang again. Annoyed, Miss Burns cupped her hand over the receiver and called out to her daughter, Marge, in the kitchen. "Marge, do you hear that bell? Go see who's at the door!"

But Marge hadn't heard the bell; she hadn't heard Miss Burns calling her, either. Marge was preoccupied, sipping coffee out in the kitchen, listening to Wendell Kinney tell some epic tales about a dance she'd missed the weekend before. Marge had known Wendell since grade school and thought him good company, nothing more. Of course, all you had to do was look into those sad, bloodhound eyes of his to know that he was crazy about Marge. Miss Burns would say, Marge, don't be leading that poor boy on! But Marge would visit with him as often as he came by. Aw, we just like to talk, she'd say to her mother, the fact being that Wendell was the local tattler, with a gift for getting secrets out of men and women alike. So, no, Marge hadn't heard nothing from the front of the house; she was too busy listening to Wendell's chortles about how big Hattie Green left the dance and climbed in the backseat of Sylvester Long's car with him, he himself being no tinier than Hattie—and how everybody knew 'bout this since it took three football players huffing and puffing to pull them out.

The doorbell rang again, and this time Miss Burns gave up on trying to rouse Marge. After promising Miss York she'd call her back, Miss Burns went to the door, smoothing her apron as she went. After opening the vestibule door, she could see through the pebbled glass of the outer door that whoever it was, bouncing around on her doormat as if he were remembering a tune, was a white man. This alerted her, and made her clear her throat and open the door cautiously. It was with her I'm-not-buying-anything-today voice that Miss Burns said to the white man before her, "Good day, and how may I help you?"

The white man did an odd thing: he took off his hat. Visibly, he composed himself. Then he said politely, "Hello, I'm Lester Cole. I'm looking for Margaret Burns. I'm, well, a friend of hers. Is this her house? Do I have the right address?"

Miss Burns stayed coiled; the man's unthreatening manner and alleged acquaintance with her daughter did not relax her one bit. Coolly, she said, "And how might you know my daughter?"

"Oh, *Mrs.* Burns," he exclaimed. "I'm so glad to meet you. I'm Lester! You know, Lester!"

Miss Burns knew she didn't know any Lesters—certainly

no white Lesters. With a cock of her head, she persisted with the question she'd asked before, "Excuse me—Lester—but how do you know my Margaret?"

It was Lester's turn to be puzzled, but it did not take him long to realize that his name wasn't ringing a bell for Miss Burns, and that that meant something was wrong. It also meant that what he'd come to the house to inquire about was going to be that much harder to accomplish. Lester decided for now just to answer Miss Burns's question. "I know Margaret from the university; we've been classmates; we took French together." Then he added, "We have lunch together all the time."

Miss Burns wrinkled her eyebrows and thought back to the spring. Yes, she remembered how Marge had taken to staying after morning classes to have lunch at the university's International House on 59th Street. She remembered, too, how they had lightly quarreled about it, with Miss Burns saying, "If I were you, I'd come home for lunch and save my quarters for a rainy day!" Marge had pleaded that she just wanted some time with her friends, and that was that—or, that was that until now! "Heavenly Father!" thought Miss Burns. Maybe Marge did say she was having lunch with a boy named Lester Cole, but who'd a thought Lester Cole was some grinning white boy?

"Why don't you come in the parlor?" she finally said to Lester, directing him to the chair across from the red one. "I'll see if Marge—Margaret—is available."

Miss Burns left the parlor and crossed the dining room, heading for the swinging door to the kitchen. When she got to the door and pushed it, it resisted; someone was right on the other side and it was Marge, with a funny little smile on her face. "Margaret," Miss Burns entoned, and Marge knew that when her mother called her Margaret something was up, "there is a Lester Cole here to see you. He's waiting in the parlor. Shall I tell him you're available?"

Wendell Kinney let out a low whistle and started a chuckle he tried to muffle. "Lester Cole here? This oughta be good!" Wendell had to hold on to the kitchen table to keep from rolling off his chair with laughter. But he sobered up right quick when he saw the look Miss Burns was giving him. "Guess I'll be on my way," Wendell said, heading for the back door out to the yard and the alley.

"Wendell!" Miss Burns hissed sharply, "don't you dare go out the back door!" Hurt, Wendell comprehended her meaning, stopped, and turned to her. "Oh, Miss Burns, don't think that; I'd never do that!"

"Then what in heaven's name *are* you doing?" she asked. Wendell became jovial again and explained, "Well, Miss Burns, I'm headed over to Michigan Avenue and it's much closer going this way."

"And why are you going to Michigan Avenue when you and I both know you live on Prairie and you ought to be getting home?"

Wendell went out the back door without replying, then stuck his head back in, saying, "'Cause I know some people over on Michigan who'd just love to know that Lester Cole is sitting up in your parlor!" Peals of Wendell's laughter descended into the yard. Marge screamed, "Wendell, don't you dare!" But Wendell was gone.

Marge and Miss Burns exchanged glances while Marge slipped out to the parlor. In Miss Burns's eyes you could see both curiosity and concern; Marge's glance said, "I can explain," though even Marge knew she didn't know where to begin. "Lester! How nice to see you!" Marge burst into the parlor smiling brilliantly, the whoosh of her petticoats a roar in Lester's ears.

"Hello, Margaret, I'm back in town," Lester began, fidgeting with his hat. "Yes! I can see that!" chimed Marge.

Miss Burns overheard that as she was peeking and listening from behind the kitchen door. "That's the dippiest thing I ever heard that girl say," she thought to herself. She peeked again and saw Lester and Marge just standing there, their mouths pursed for speech, but nothing was coming out.

Then Marge said brightly, "I know, I've got an idea! Let's us go around the corner to Walgreen's and have a cup of coffee! We can catch up!" Swiftly, Marge grabbed up her sweater and pocketbook, and steered Lester by his elbow to the front door before he could mumble a word. Once in the vestibule, Marge yelled, "Momma! We're going out for coffee! I'll be back soon!"

Miss Burns heard the door slam shut and retreated back into the kitchen. She puttered around doing little things like placing the salt and pepper shakers back where they should be. Mainly, she was collecting her thoughts, rehearsing all that had just transpired. When she set to clearing the cups and saucers Marge and Wendell had just used, it occurred to her Marge had just had coffee; now, she was skipping out the door for more coffee, and with a white boy. That got Miss Burns to shaking her head. "I don't think I'm going to call York back just yet," she mused. "And what am I going to tell Ocie?" Then she started wiping clean a counter that was already spotless.

———

Two blocks away on 58th Street, Marge and Lester found a little table in the Walgreen's cafeteria. Marge ordered a small ice cream sundae while Lester got a sandwich, grilled ham on raisin toast. Talk came easier than it had in Miss Burns's parlor; it was as if it were spring quarter at the university all over again, and they were again meeting for lunch at the International House.

"I didn't realize you lived around the corner from Morry's," Lester exclaimed. "That's great!" Lester knew all about Morry's, the best jazz record store in the city. He had probably been in Morry's hundreds of times more than any of the Burnses. Just mentioning Morry's got Lester going, his head dipping, his thumbs thumping a rhythm on the table's edge. Marge was amused as she always was, but this time only for an instant. Oh Lester, my crazy Lester, she thought, we're in a world of trouble and you're sitting here, fingerpopping.

"We need to talk — seriously, I mean." Marge reached over to silence Lester's thumping, trying not to frown. Lester stopped thumping and Marge quickly retracted her hand; they didn't need to be looking like they were holding hands, she thought.

Lester looked Marge in the eye, really for the first time that day. "You haven't told your folks about me, have you?"

"No."

"I mean," Lester continued, "I just met your mother and said 'Hi, I'm Lester' and she looked at me like I was nutty or something." Marge fluttered her hand as if to say what did you expect.

Lester peered at Marge a while. "What have you told them?"

"Nothing much."

Lester sighed and looked about the store. "I thought we had a plan," he began. "We were going to go to Evanston and get married, then I was going to take that dance band job up at Lake Delavan for the summer, and that was going to give you two whole months to talk to your folks and get things straight. What happened?"

"Well," Marge replied, "we did get married."

"Yeah," said Lester, starting to grin, "and I went up to Lake Delavan. But you know what I mean."

Marge tried to frame a reasonable reply, but all she could muster was, "I tried to talk with them but I couldn't find the right moment."

"In two months? There wasn't a moment in two whole months?" Lester sounded angry, and Marge searched for anger in his face but couldn't really find it. "Were you scared?" asked Lester.

"Yes."

"Were you having second thoughts?" Lester tried to get Marge to look at him when he asked this.

"Maybe." Marge played with her ice cream with her spoon.

Suddenly feeling cornered and put upon, Marge snapped, "Wait a minute, Lester, what about you? Did you tell your folks—or did you just run away to Lake Delavan?"

Lester wiped the corners of his mouth with his napkin. "I told them; I told them while I was packing to go. I said, 'I got to tell you something before I take off.' I said, 'I just got married to a girl I've been dating at school, and you might as well know she's colored.'"

Aghast, Marge asked, "What did they say?"

"Well, Poppa said, '*How* colored?'" Lester grinned. "But Ma started screaming."

Marge stared at Lester, then she stared some more. Lester rattatated a new rhythm along his edge of the table.

"Stop that!" Marge hissed. Lester folded his hands in his lap like a choir boy and looked up at her. "I can't believe you told them!" Lester shrugged. "And your mother started screaming?" Marge's eyes were as big as coasters.

"Yeah, and then she started cursing and wailing in Polish; all around the house, in and out of my room, yelling in Polish."

Marge had forgotten that Lester was Polish. He didn't look Polish or sound Polish, though Marge admitted that she wasn't sure exactly what a Pole should look or sound like. She remembered that Lester had told her that he had changed his name to Cole from Kowalski because he thought that would help his jazz career. He had said, grinning, "Hey! Maybe they'll think I'm one of the Coles, like Cozy Cole or Nat King Cole!" She knew then that he was not just lovable but as goofy as they come.

"So, how did you leave it with them?" Marge asked. "I mean, where did things stand when you left for Lake Delavan?"

"Not too good." Lester was squirming around in his chair. "Poppa's OK—he's kinda intrigued, if you know what I mean. But Ma said, 'When you get back from Wisconsin, you better go live with your new wife, 'cause you ain't living here!'"

Marge absorbed this; this was precisely the kind of scenario she herself was dreading. "So, she kicked you out of the house?"

"Yep."

"So, where are you living?"

"That's what I got to talk with you about."

Marge took a deep breath; Lester did the same—it seemed like good idea. "Lester, you can't possibly be thinking of living with me."

"Yes I am."

"'Cause there's no way I can leave Momma and Daddy—and I want to finish college!"

"I know, I know."

"So, what are you thinking of?"

"Well, I sorta thought maybe I could move in with you and your folks—as a boarder of course."

"No!"

"Why not?"

"No. No-no-no-no, no."

"C'mon. I'm in a jam."

"Can't you think of somewhere else to go?"

"No."

"Why?"

"'Cause I'm your husband, and I want to be near you."

Marge had been in messes before, like the time she was engaged to *two* fellows at once, but this situation with Lester was the ultimate nightmare. She liked Lester, and for almost a year at the university she couldn't have imagined not seeing him most every day. It had been different with Lester—no games, no pressures—precisely because romance was unthinkable. They had probably been giving each other little tugs and shoves for weeks before Marge noticed it. But she dismissed it: this was Lester! Then they found themselves in the library stacks one day, way down a dim corridor, and they kissed. It wasn't too long after that they wanted to go on real dates, but that was impossible.

So, what did they do about it? They got married, and spent the first of their afternoons together in a friend's borrowed apartment. There would be three more afternoons before Lester went off to Lake Delavan. Then there would be the months leading up to now.

Marge had spent the summer, not unwillingly, in the bosom of her family and in the pleasant round of picnics and parties her world provided. She had even gone out a few times with fellows she was *supposed* to be going out with. That's how Wendell Kinney had found out about Lester. Wendell hadn't pried the secret out of Marge, it had just come gushing out. They had been to the show at the Regal and were sitting on the Burnses' porch when suddenly Marge started quivering, then crying softly, then talking. On she talked, and Wendell listened with both horror and awe. "Don't tell me you did this! You're jivin' me!" he whistled. Then he listened some more, so intent he was pointing like a hunting dog.

When Marge was done and he had consoled her all he could, Wendell had had one more piece of advice. "'Course, you and Lester could always go to France and have lots of polka-dot babies and drink wine and live the good life! That's what Josephine Baker did! That's what Willie Bates did, too — you remember Willie? 'Course, Willie's case is a little different on account of he's a sissy."

"You're crazy, Wendell, plumb crazy!" Marge was giggling now, even while she mopped up tears. "I'm crazy? *I'm* crazy?" Wendell exclaimed. "Now, that's surely the pot calling the kettle black!"

As Lester sat there across from Marge, awash in the silence between them, he was thinking about the summer as well. After descending the train and hiking through the gates of the resort at Lake Delavan, he had been struck by how *white* the place was—whiter than the university, white like the North Shore country clubs where he occasionally played in bands. The resort had a decent-size orchestra, with no colored players, of course, but it had three immigrant-boy musicians, including Lester, who might as well have been the colored help.

Between sets, the band regulars would tell nigger jokes, wop jokes, Jew jokes. When Abe Stein, a west-side Chicago boy from Benny Goodman's neighborhood, didn't laugh, they got pissed off and picked on him. The bandleader had more couth, but one day during a rehearsal he threw a fit and started cursing. Pointing at the immigrant boys, who all happened to be in the reed section, he screamed, "Goddammit! Stop playing black!"

Lester almost laughed in his face, but didn't—he needed the job. For the rest of the summer, Lester played like he was back in high school. Abe and the other boy, Tony Esposito, knew what Lester was doing, for they were doing it, too.

Lester and Tony got along at first; they talked. Lester never got around to telling Tony his name was really Kowalski, but he did tell Tony about Marge. Tony kept Lester's secret from the rest of the band, but Lester was never sure he should have confided in Tony. Tony was hard on him; Tony would say things like, "So, you think you're gonna play better, now? You think you're gonna get some tips from Coleman Hawkins?"

Then there was the day Lester socked Tony. As they

walked away from each other, both hurting, Lester heard someone complain, "Why do they hire these Chicago toughs? What's this resort coming to?" Lester knew he and Tony weren't toughs, but he also knew Tony had gone too far. "Hey, you think you're Mezz Mezzrow? What 'cha gonna do now, take your gal and move to Harlem?" Lester hit him after that. Marge was no "gal."

Marge and Lester looked at each other. "I know I was supposed to tell my parents, Lester, but I can't talk about this yet with anyone but you. Your taking that resort job seemed like a good idea, but what happened was that you went off right when we needed to be talking to each other, figuring things out. It's funny, we're married, but right now I think we knew each other better when we weren't married."

Marge sighed and looked out the window. It was a sunny afternoon, but the sunlight was thinner, weaker; fall was approaching.

"I don't want to lose you," Lester began. "I'm not going to push you into anything, but I'm not going to walk away either. I want to give us a try. We can't live together just yet, but I can't go back to seeing you every other day for lunch—I just can't!"

"Nor can I," Marge whispered. "Uncle Fred moved out of the spare room last month. I can point out that we've boarded college students before. School begins in a week. Your housing fell through. You don't need a place for the whole year, just for the first term."

"Yeah," Lester said. "We met at the International House. I'm a foreign student still learning the ways of this country. I'm a little lonely, being so far away from my Ma-ma and Papa. I need to be with a good family, eating home-cooked meals."

"Stop it."

"I need to be around the corner from Morry's where I can buy that good American *jazz* music!"

"Lester! Stop it!"

Lester stopped, and slid his hand across the table. Marge placed her hand in his. They were holding hands and it didn't matter who saw.

"Walk me home, Lester, Miss Burns is going to be worrying." Lester stood up and gave a little bow. "I'm at your service, Margaret."

Marge whooshed her petticoats, Lester grinned that grin of his, and they were off.

III

Blue as the Lake

ABOVE: *Ocie Burns on camel,*
circa 1905.

Black Piano

Here now in its Connecticut home, the black piano nestles in a corner of the dining room, which I like to call the music corner. On the surrounding walls are musical images: Della Robbia's Florentine dancing youths, Vincent Smith's print, "Riding on a Blue Note: 'Round Midnight." Atop the piano, besides the mail order catalogs which get dumped there, and the trays of cassettes which should be better housed closer to the audio equipment, are piles of music from three generations of family, music that just stuck to the piano like filings to a black magnet, and traveled with it into the present.

Poke in a pile and you'll find Grandma Burns's *The New Blue Book of Favorite Songs*, "new" in 1941, nearly an heirloom now. A little more digging unearths my mother's telephone book–size collection of Beethoven Sonatas for the Pianoforte, with her college address and sorority affiliation (she was a Delta) neatly inked on the cover. My sister hasn't played this piano since the 1960s, and yet I find Kris Stepto's (she was "Kris" not Jan for about three adolescent years) *Chopin*

Waltzes. My wife Michele and I didn't know each other when she was studying music in college, and yet Michele's *Bach Riemenschneider* is here with everything else, still tagged with a Stanford textbook sticker. And our boys: the music for piano and violin is Gabe's (he and Michele worked their way up to Vitale) and the bright red booklets with titles like *Teaching Little Fingers to Play* are Rafe's. These are relics, memories, of the preteen days before both boys, now young men, took up the acoustic guitar.

I, too, was a player of this piano and yet none of my sheet music remains. You will just have to believe that when I studied piano in the 1950s, with the teacher provided me, boys learned not the simpler Bach and such but items like the "Marines' Hymn" and countless cowboy songs, "Red River Valley," for example. I'm not there on top of the piano except perhaps in what a back issue or two of *Living Blues* might signify. Sometimes I vow that during my next leave from the university I will return to the piano; that when Mr. Deutsch comes in September to tune the piano after a summer's humidity, it will be a tuning for me, too. Perhaps that will happen this year. Meanwhile, I listen to Rafe play, amused by his new mutterings about "mastering" this instrument. Sometimes he impresses me with new sounds, new workings-out of something he is also exploring on guitar. Other times I am confounded by what it might all mean that all 6'2" of him is pouring itself into remembered exercises for "little fingers." What exactly is he remembering?

The piano arrived in New Haven in 1976 to our Chapel Street house, my mother having sent it to us along with a few pieces of outdoor furniture when she and my father moved to the high-rise apartment she would live in the rest of her life. I knew why they had no need of the outdoor furniture anymore, but the inclusion of the piano was a mystery. The apartment is spacious, especially in its living room; the piano, a special Steinway model designed for apartments, could have fitted most anywhere. And I don't think that being on the 28th floor was a real deterrent: professional movers can carefully move a piano anywhere, especially if the piano is compact. But the piano came our way, and we gratefully took it in, my feelings being quite like those when an aunt recently sent me all her family photos: if I am the one she wants to have these precious things, then so be it.

But I must admit that I wondered then, and am still wondering, what my mother had in mind in giving up her piano. How could she do this when music, piano, had been so important during at least the first thirty years of her life, and when we all knew what buying the piano for her had meant to my father?

When my parents married at a young age, my father promised that he would buy my mother a fine piano as soon as he was able. This happened roughly ten years later, medical school and everything else, including me and my sister, intervening. Twenty years after that, the piano is banished to Connecticut, along with some furniture. How come? What sort of rearrangement was being orchestrated, what beginning—or end—asserted? Here are some images I keep reeling through, pieces to a puzzle I'm not sure I want to solve.

1939. Coleman Hawkins is back from Europe and now in town, playing a club or maybe a big dance hall. He calls his cousin, Ocie, my mother's father, and it is arranged that he will come out to the house for Sunday dinner. Immediately afterward there are the usual conversations. The children squeal and whisper, excited about the visit, and proudly slip the news to neighbors, some of whom plan to just happen to be outside, sitting or sweeping or dusting a car, just get a glimpse of the Hawk. The adults begin with memories, Missouri memories: of vexed and vexing great-grandmother Maggie Hawkins Burns; of her husband, Smith Burns, "lighting out for the territory," leaving her and the race for life in Colorado; of her brother, Will, Coleman's father, ending his life by walking into the Missouri River one frosty February morning, his pipe still lit and glowing as he fiercely waded deeper and deeper—tired, so tired, of being a shipping clerk at American Electrical and a "credit to his race" (as reported in the obituary), and maybe tired of his family, too.

After rehearsing the miseries then come the anxieties: What is Coleman going to bring to our door? Will he be drunk? Will he smell of that reefer? Will we be keeping the Sabbath with that man here? Are we thinking of the children?

My mother's stories, full of remembered annoyance and exasperation, paint this sort of picture. For her part, she wanted Coleman to visit; she wanted to be with the one musician in the family who played something other than hymns and knew about the music she was studying; after all, he had started out on the cello. On the other hand, she was terrified, for surely there would be the moment when her father would insist that she play for Coleman. Because he had been so removed from the inner workings of the family, she had no idea whether he would be a supportive or cruelly devastating listener.

The day came, Coleman sauntered into the Burns house, and so came the moment when Anna had to play. My guess is that Coleman, moderately sober, played it cool, listened to the Bach or whatever, picked a path between offering congratulations and offering a few pointers, smoked a cigarette and looked for dessert. My mother remembered that day most complexly. At the same time that it pitted her against her parents as Coleman's champion and apologist, so too did it seal her fate as a music major in college. As my grandfather had chosen careers for his older children, so too had he resolutely chosen Anna's. After high school, she would enter the music school at Northwestern; there really was no discussion about it.

Being a practical man who had just lived through the Depression, Ocie didn't exactly let Anna go up to Evanston and major solely in piano (though the extra fees for practice room times were cheerfully paid). She majored in music education and prepared for a career as an elementary school music teacher. But the stories that last from those times are all about music and performers of music: about Kay Davis who went on briefly to sing with Duke Ellington; about Ann De Ramus, later to be named my godmother, who actually tried to make it as a concert pianist in New York and struggled and starved and didn't make it but thank God found and married a nice man; about Bill Komaiko, the one true sweet white guy in the music school who once took Anna to the movies only for them to be rudely turned away at the door by the manager. (Incredibly, years later, Bill Jr. would be a cabinmate of mine at YMCA camp.) And there are the stories, countless stories, about the grinding routines forced by the commute (blacks couldn't live in the dorms at Northwestern until fifteen years later) and by the need to practice, and practice.

Anna rose at five each morning in order to get to the El

stop at 58th Street by six. If the trains were on time, she was out to Evanston and in a classroom or practice room by eight. The rest of the day was a predictable mix of class, practice, study. After dinner, Anna went to the library and studied until it closed at eight (I think of this every time some of today's students petition to have the libraries stay open beyond midnight). Then came the two-hour commute back home. "The time just skipped along," she would tell me, "because I usually was deep into the piece of music I was reading. I read music all the time just like other people on the train would be reading newspapers."

Perhaps she was still deep into a sonata the night her usual alertness was switched off, and she found herself on 58th Street, terrified by a man looking for more than money. Just when it descended on her that she might not get away, a man as big as a truck stepped out of the shadows and said ever so softly, "This man botherin' you. Anna?" It was a boy, now monstrously grown, with whom she had gone to grade school. He walked her home that evening, and often doffed his hat to her in evenings to come—for as regularly as she came home from school he was perpetually hanging around the pool hall.

This was one of my mother's "how determined I was to get an education" stories. It was also one of the stories that helped paint how dangerous 58th Street could be—why it was called the "bucket of blood." But I see now, especially with its good samaritan sprung from the halls of an inner-city grade school, that this was a story to help explain why my mother would soon teach in the toughest schools on the South Side: those are kids to help, not avoid; those are kids who just might help *you* some day.

The 1940s were years of milestones and achievements for my mother, but so too were they years of frustration and struggle, especially once she was settled into the certainty of the justness of her resentments. In 1942, she married but did so against the wishes of her father, who wanted her to wait until she had finished college and my father had completed medical school. After the September ceremony ("the great elopement with us totally oblivious to the fact that it was the *13th* of the month," my mother would later write), she had to inhabit the realities of returning to college while being married to a man seven hundred miles away, and living out the self-inflicted torments that would come, at least for a while, when she saw her father's face. It was doubtlessly in that context, that brew of autumn weather, that a photographer came and took the remarkable large photograph of my mother in a wedding dress, beautifully posed on the landing of the steps of her father's house. Though not as much of a fiction as a huge, after-the-fact wedding would have been, the photo was still an airy concoction, and my mother knew it. While she laughed about it, she learned how to brood about it, too. Once in our house, once we had a house, the photo was never hidden, never hung, either.

Probably in 1945 or 1946, after my father had returned to Chicago to start his internships and residencies, after the birthing of me, and after she had earned both her bachelor's and master's degrees from Northwestern, my mother sought a teaching position in the Chicago public schools. This she did with mounting urgency: with her husband earning less than $100 a month as an intern and with all of us crowded into her parents' house, she had to find work.

A job did not come easily, and not just because the schools like the factories were hiring back the men returning from soldiering in the war. It didn't help that she was inexperienced, only twenty-two, and looked younger. And while she thought that her Northwestern education would be an asset, a driving wedge, it turned out to be a question mark, even a curse. In interview after interview, the functionaries in charge of hiring were abundantly clear that they were also in charge of protecting the "interests" (their term was *standards*) of the city's public teacher's colleges. My mother would sit in a reception area, neat and proper in just the right skirt and blouse, fidgeting with her résumé, reviewing what to play on the piano if asked to play, only to be brought into the interview and be told, "We think you studied too much piano," or, "Northwestern's courses really don't prepare you for teaching our children," and, "You should have gone to teacher's college, right here in Chicago—that's where our best teachers come from." At some turn in the corridors of this idiocy, before employment came and the frustrations abated, my mother must have thought about how she ended up at Northwestern in the first place, who insisted, who virtually filled out the application. She learned then how to twist her piano-trained fingers into fists, and how to release them before returning home.

I don't recall all the schools where my mother taught before taking a maternity leave in 1952 to have my sister, never to return to the classroom. But they were all rugged, draining, heart-of-the-ghetto assignments, possibly given to my mother to "toughen her up," or because they were undesirable to anyone with the seniority to be elsewhere. Raymond School, a sullen mound of brick near 39th and State, stands foremost for me, partly because of my mother's stories of it,

and partly because it has occurred to me that if Richard
Wright's Bigger Thomas really had lived at 37th and Indiana
(his address in *Native Son*) he would have attended elementary
school at Raymond. And indeed the two sets of stories,
Wright's and my mother's, converge: her stories of Raymond
School were tales of classrooms full of Biggers, and of their
mothers (even then only their mothers) marching up to the
school either to wring their hands or get hotly right up in
your face.

In my mother's stories, the biggest, baddest, most bonafide
Biggers were girls, especially a girl I will call Darlene. One
afternoon, after disciplining Darlene (one time too many as
far as Darlene was concerned), my mother returned to the
blackboard and to the rest of the lesson. From behind her she
heard gasps, foot scrapings. Turning around, there was Darlene, sharpening her eyes, twitching with rage, brandishing a
knife. Dropping the chalk, my mother lunged at the teacher's
desk and grabbed up a pair of eight-inch shears. Then it
started. Darlene war-stepped closer, whispering, "I'm sick of
your shit." My mother hissed, "C'mon little bitch. C'mon."
When they were close, when only six feet of honeywood floor
remained between them, my mother raised her weapon but
went for her words, for that precious pint of trashtalk she car-
ried for emergencies. "C'mon, little bitch. C'mon and try and
take me. These shears gonna mess you up long before you
even think of what you trying to do with that knife. You see
me you see teacher. What you don't see, 'cause you don't know
nuthin', is that I am from 58th Street, bucket of blood. You
want to know why they call it the bucket of blood? Then
c'mon."

Darlene was dangerous. In another time—our sorry era,

for instance—she would have wasted my mother (maybe because she would have had a gun, and you don't have to walk those last few feet to use a gun). But Darlene backed down, whispering something about "another time." That was it. There may have been the rest of the day to contend with—a now irrelevant teachers' meeting, the decision whether to report Darlene, a fearful walk to where she had parked her small gray car. But the brush with harm or worse marked the end of my mother's story and, though not with perfect logic, the end of her days as a music teacher. After Darlene and the knife, mother went back to school and retrained herself as a reading specialist. While there was much that was admirable in this re-dedication, this brave new marshaling of forces to make a difference, so too was there something horrible: a ghetto school had lost a music teacher, and that teacher, my mother, was suddenly long down the road to removing the practice of music from her life. Darlene's knife had nicked her after all.

But the piano arrived anyway. It was black—not some nonsense, bleached-out, decor-coordinating shade, but classically and classily black. Even before you opened the hinged keyboard cover and watched the gold lettering scroll into view, you knew it was something fine, a Steinway. As if built to the purpose, it fitted snugly along the left wall of our apartment's foyer, giving the space function and a kind of quiet glamour. The piano gathered unto it many tiny groupings of gazers and strokers. Everyone sensed that this was a special instrument, special to my mother and father and their marriage. No one, least of all my mother, dreamt that such an elegant fulfillment of my father's promises might also be the first, forming articulations of something else.

Once the piano came, music lessons for me were inevitable.

I was soon jostled off to a school near 63rd Street in what had been a two-flat building like our own. Saturday mornings I found myself first in what still looked like a parlor, bored and fractious in the midst of dullards taking weeks to comprehend the difference between half and quarter notes. But I always got my comeuppance when it came time to descend to the basement practice rooms, for while I could read music, playing it was mysteriously another matter. After the recital in which I maniacally stormed through the "Marines' Hymn," my mother and I cut a deal: I could quit the piano if I agreed to art lessons at the Art Institute.

Children want to please their parents and yearn to avoid those activities in which they cannot shine—or worse, in which they disappoint. I hated being so plodding at the piano, hated my mother's dismay, hated every syllable of encouragement which exposed her distress instead of veiling it. Thank God my art teacher at school had given me a little, one-bulletin-board show and had said I had talent. It was a terrible thing to do poorly something your mother did well; now I had a way out of that.

Relief came to me, not so to my mother: in one of her first acts of providing for her children better than she provided for herself, she released me from the black piano while subjecting herself to what were its increasing demands. While I went off to the Art Institute School each Saturday, she daily sat down to play, thundering out scales upon scales before taking up a piece of music, Chopin or something Chopinesque. It sounded fine to me, even transporting. But no sooner were you into it than it stopped, right in the middle of a run. From my room or the end of the hall I could hear small human sounds, the yips and yelps that well-brought-up ladies like my mother substitute for curses, before they decide to curse. I never got too close, never inched up the hall for a better view of the fits. Perhaps because I had done my own bout with that piano I never said something stupid like, "What's the matter?" But I got more than an eyeful that time she freight-trained down the hall, blazing, smoking. As she passed, so swift she sucked the air from the apartment, I heard her say, "I used to *play* that." The black piano gleamed in the near distance. I couldn't take my eyes off it.

After 1960, my mother never played the piano, as far as I know. But music never left her life: she eagerly anticipated going to the opera and symphony, and she would plan all year for the Memorial Weekend galas back in the halcyon time when my father's club, the Chicagoans, would import Duke Ellington or Count Basie for days of serious partying. (How well I remember her breathlessly telling me, from some pay phone in some hotel, that Paul Gonsalves had just soloed even better than he did on "Crescendo in Blue" on the Ellington at Newport album.) It was she who got us kids off to school in the morning, literally bopping and swinging. We listened on the radio to both the "white" jazz station with the hipster disc jockey who read off the baseball scores—five to two, six to four, one to nothing—with no mention of the teams, and to the "black" station that featured Daddy-O Daylie, the legendary announcer whom Cannonball Adderley honored with his tune, "Blues for Daddy-O." Many a recording came in the house because of a cut we had heard at seven in the morning, trying to wake up on the right side of the bed.

Music, jazz, was a late-night affair for my mother. It was especially in the evening, with my father so often away, that in

Michael Harper's words, "the music, *jazz*, came in." A few vocalists would pay a visit—Ella, Sarah, Johnny Hartman, Frank and Tony—Miles, Paul Desmond, and Clifford Brown were always welcome. Summers in Michigan with my father two hundred miles away in Chicago, these were her companions, their tunes my lullabies. Later when we remained in Chicago for the summer, I installed some weatherproof speakers so that music could waft the patio, fantasizing only as teenagers can do of sunny picnics and soft-night parties with slow-dancing under the moon. Never did I anticipate that this would ease my mother into sitting alone outdoors into the night, drinking, thinking, forever caressing the edge of some exquisite solo. I see her now, shivering, listening to Sarah sing "September Song" to Quincy Jones's arrangements, telling me she needs just a little more time on the patio before the autumn leaves begin to fade, shuddering in the sharpening Chicago winds, shaking with each descent of Sarah's notes into the lower registers.

Recently, while talking about my mother with my sons, I badly needed a hit of her, needed the sight of her tall thin brown self, swinging, fingerpopping, schooling me in what to listen for. For reasons having to do with beginnings, with our first improvisations into companionship, I sought and found "Workin'" (Prestige, 1956), remembering how much my mother loved Miles's solo on "It Never Entered My Mind." The LP didn't deliver: too many scratches, primitive audio, nothing to bring back my mother. I sat in my chair defeated—only that word will do—then Gabe touched me on the shoulder as he will, saying, "Wait a minute," and he ran upstairs. Returning, he slipped in a tape and a perfect recording of "Workin'" filled the room. He said, "A guy down the hall at

Brown had this; I copied it." I said, "I haven't heard this without the scratches in twenty years."

Gabe went out to meet some friends. I settled back and played the tape again, finding "It Never Entered My Mind" complete with Miles's solo and Red Garland's tinklings. Then my mother came in, dancing past the black piano, finger-popping.

Hyde Park

All my flights from the East to Chicago end this way. After an indifferent run across uniform southern Michigan farmland, we burst upon the blue expanse of Lake Michigan, momentarily as big as any sea one must cross to get to a place completely unknown. Then the pilot comes on the intercom: We're descending, we're arriving soon, the wind is windy, the Cubs are losing, have a good day. Some passengers moan and wonder: Descent? Did he say descent? Good God we're over water. I thought we were going to Chicago.

While they shift and lurch and try to remember the instructions half-heard two hours before about flotation devices, I ease back and almost say out loud: the Lake looks good to me. A hit of the Lake before landing in the prairie's drift and then driving into the humid heft of the city is just what I need. I romanticize the Lake. Even though I know and even dream the tales of the Lake's dangers—ore ships vanishing, nice people like my fourth-grade teacher drowning—I still want to be out there, nudging through the Lake's waves. Riding to

nowhere with my dad in Dr. Calloway's powerboat at six in
the morning with only a sack of chocolate donuts for breakfast and only a thin White Sox jacket to shell off the fog
and breeze—that's where I want to be. Riding the ferry from
Milwaukee to Ludington on a sunny childhood day, playing shuffleboard during the few intervals the ship's captain
doesn't need my helmsmanship—that's not bad, either. Aching with hope that the one man in my father's crowd with a
sailboat, a fast yawl no less, might ask me to help crew in the
next Chicago to Mackinac race—that's a first-rate might-
have-been, an outstanding almost-happened.

But then we land and it's time to get down to business,
the business of getting out to the South Side. Years ago, provided that I wasn't traveling with my wife—who is deeply
suspicious of my homegrown itineraries—I'd plan elaborate
schemes of travel, with transfers, double-transfers, and the
like. It was just no fun and much too adult simply to hail a cab
and debark at home forty-five minutes later. I'd claim that I
couldn't afford a cab, but what I really couldn't afford was de-
priving myself of a short wade into the city's essences.

These days, I grab a cab more and more, chiefly because the
cabdrivers are more interesting. Gone, it seems, are the sullen
rednecks who resent driving you anywhere; gone, too, are the
tiresome black cabbies who want to know "How many coloreds are up to that college you go to?" or want to borrow ten
dollars—"I know your address and everything, you know I'll
pay you back." No, these days you get the West Indian and
East Indian and even West African types: brothers with cabs
like living rooms, smelling like sweet flowers, decked out with
photographs, doilies, little national flags and no smoking
signs in three languages. These brothers have coolers with

sodas and iced cappucinos; when they offer a cold drink they add, "Would you like my business card, too?" I like these dudes because they make you think uplift and hustle are still the order of the day. But these guys are new to Chicago. There's another reality, too, dancing not to the hustle but to the blues.

The "blues ride," the "nachal" ride full of testiness and style and eruptions of funk, comes not in the rolling parlors of the new American dreamers but instead in the utilitarian vans of the A2B Coach Company, a black-owned outfit that serves the University of Chicago by way of stopping half a dozen places where black folks might want to go. There's a published route with designated times, but like a Gershwin tune that's caught the eye of Sonny Rollins, it's a score about to be improvised upon. Frankly, I don't worry any more when the van gets to 22nd Street and then suddenly veers west for blocks. The driver ain't crazy, ain't lost; someone's slipped him a five to drop them off in Chinatown, and that's what's happening. And don't let a doe-eyed stewardess sweetly step aboard, show some leg, and let it drop that she lives in an apartment in Lake Meadows. Lake Meadows never was on the schedule—but it is now.

The last time I rode out to the South Side before my father died, I deliberately took an A2B van, even though the next one wasn't going to leave for almost an hour. My father had been acting oddly—had even sent me a postcard the week before suggesting I not come—and so I actually welcomed the delay. Why rush things? Why beat a path to his apartment only to lengthen the time in which you tensely had to wait for him to come home with whatever was really on his mind?

Predictably, the first folk arriving and peering around for

the A2B were white and heading for the university. Going to see my fiancée, said one; considering the medical school, said two more. I nodded and tried to judge from their clothes what parts of the country they were from. Next, a dapper coffee-colored man strode up, decked out in sport clothes and soft leather shoes. He saw me smoking—I had to get that done before meeting my father—and asked me for a light. As his left hand motored in spiraling circles, he put one foot out in front of the other and told me he was a judge. (I much wanted to believe him.) Told me that sometimes he just had to get out of town. Told me how he would slip into his chambers, change clothes, grab his overnight bag, go down the service elevator to the street, and then high-step over to the El train that went out to O'Hare and, you know, be Gone. He asked if I had ever taken that El train; told me to try it sometime.

The A2B came and we all clambered aboard, the last-minute arrivals including a wizened black couple wearing church clothes—I couldn't help placing them however unfairly as the couple in the eviction scene in Ellison's *Invisible Man*—and a heavy-set brown woman, exquisitely dressed, who I instantly knew would be the van's "other driver." She squeezed in next to me, humming, and dabbing her faint perspiration in an elegant manner worthy of Ella or Sarah.

We weren't too far into Hillary Clinton's neighborhood of Park Ridge before everybody heard from the lady next to me. "Mister Driver? Mister Driver? Do you think you could turn up the air-conditioning?" Now, it was a cool day and the air-conditioning wasn't even on. But the driver, even though he was too young to have been of the old school of waiter's waiters or porter's porters, was accommodating. After blues-lining out something about how he hadn't turned on no air-

conditioner on the thirty-goddamn-first of March in all his
born days, he mellowed and told some lie about how A2B
Coach always wants to please. The chill hit the elderly couple
instantly. Their skin ashened as they hunched into their winter coats.

Pretty soon we all were cold to the bone. I looked over at
the clutch of white folks, shuddering like they were back in
North Dakota, and could see in their eyes that they were just
going to shut their mouths and ride this one out. Clearly, they
feared that one little word would bring an NAACP lawsuit, or
worse, the signifying wrath of the lady next to me. No, white
folks weren't going to bail us out this time. I looked for the
judge; thought I might see him righteously agitated, and cold,
too. But the judge was dozing—or pretending to doze. I understood: if the brother had been telling the truth all along, he
didn't need to get in a fracas on the A2B while sneaking back
to his courtroom. So, it was up to me.

Before I opened my mouth, my whole history in Chicago
flew by me. I asked myself for the umpteenth time why I had
left and why I always came back. I asked myself what I loved
and what I dreaded. Then I asked myself why I was pondering
these things when all I had to do was to say, "Excuse me, I'm
cold, all these people are cold, please turn the cooling down."
But it came out another way: "Mr. Driver, sir," I said, echoing
the lady but adding my own flourish, "could we please have
some heat?"

The white folks were grateful; the elderly black couple
murmured, "Amen." You couldn't tell about the dozing judge,
but I thought I saw a smile. We waited for the lady next to me
to explode, but she surprised us by saying, "You know, I
thought it was cold. This bus is cold." And she started hum-

ming again. All was peaceful for a jot until the driver likely lost his mind. "Y'all want air-conditioning," he said, "Y'all want heat. Y'all don't know what you want, don't never know what you want." So it was coming, not from the lady next to me but from the driver, and it was coming. I thought we were going to hear about Mississippi next, as he began to careen the van down the expressway. But I was wrong: the tune was in the key of Arkansas. "Been up to this city for thirty years," he began. The old couple whispered, "O Lord." "Been here driving every kind of car, cab, truck, van, what have you." "Please," I said. "But this job a motherfucka," he swore. "'Bout time I got back to Arkansas."

From Roosevelt Road to Oakwood Boulevard, we heard about Arkansas. The landscape the driver painted—each tug at the steering wheel another swipe of his brush—had nothing to do with civil rights and troops and Little Rock and Governor Faubus and what trouble must have been at his door thirty, forty years ago. It was more like that Archibald Motley painting, "Landscape-Arkansas," a pretty scene from a dream. I couldn't hear all he said, the big lady next to me kept whispering nonsense at me, but I heard something about fishing and buttermilk. And there was the part about growing turnip greens and collards out in the garden. The driver's voice got louder and gruff when he told us about how in Arkansas, "Black folks *knows* when they wants hot, and *knows* when they wants cold." Then he half-turned his head and said, "And the white folks are *comprehensible!*" Comprehensible? Com-pre-hensible?? That fifty-dollar word made me wonder if the driver were a preacher on the side.

I got off the van at Hyde Park's Ramada Inn, curious about what else was in store for the rest of the passengers, maybe especially the white folks, as they rode deeper into the South Side. After brushing off the cabbies eager for a fare, I shouldered my bags and started walking the two long blocks to my father's apartment building. I was walking through an area called Indian Village, so-called because the high-rise buildings had names like Blackhawk and Mohican. As a boy, I used to be invited to birthday parties by white classmates living in the Blackhawk or some such apartment house and have a heck of a time getting past the white doorman until my friend's mother or father came down in the elevator, all flushed and sorry, to get me. I was walking and thinking about all that, and realizing that I didn't care about that anymore. Or rather, I didn't care about it half as much as I cared about the trepidations of walking a block further and entering the building in which my mother and her mother had lived their last days, leaving my father behind, much to his astonishment, confusion, and anger, too. Of entering that building, of struggling through the revolving door with my bags jostling me, there was but one verity: the people manning the door, and even those vacuuming the lobby and supervising with their clipboards, were going to hail me and maybe hug me, too. And I would hug them back. After that, I was on my own, seeking the elevator to the 28th floor, settling into the apartment in which I had never really lived but which had been the family's home for almost twenty years. Then came the wait for my father, who was a long time coming.

Even after putting up with the A2B Coach and its meandering path to the South Side, I still got out to my father's place a full hour before we were supposed to meet there. Borrowing the keys left for me with the doorman, I let myself into the apartment, my head bobbing from side to side, not because I expected to find someone waiting for me, but because I was already curious about what might have changed and what had been left untouched in the three years since my mother had died. Nothing much caught my eye until I went into the bathroom my mother had come to use more and more instead of the one off her bedroom. The cosmetics were gone, the pills were gone; the myriad items for doing hair and painting nails and all the rest were gone. I said to myself, "Maybe he's gotten around to doing something about her clothes, too." But I didn't look to see.

What I did do was look for the family photo albums that had been on my mind ever since I had planned this trip. I wanted to find the photo of my grandfather astride a camel in Egypt with the Sphinx in the background; it was taken in 1905, back when he must have thought that life had more in store for him than endless shifts at the post office. I was looking, too, for my mother's wedding picture, so beautiful yet so contrived since there had never been a wedding with a flowing gown and a groom handsome in a cutaway but instead a rushed, almost secret ceremony, to be confessed to later.

There were two other photos I was burning to find. One documented my father's initiation into his college fraternity. Clipped from the pages of the Chicago *Defender*, it offered a youthful image of my father I did not wish to forget, and it provided proof of something very interesting to me even though it had never been talked about in the family: my father was initiated in the same group with the novelist Frank Yerby—and so my father must have known Yerby, and maybe my mother did too.

The other photo was one of me at three years old. Frankly,

I liked it as an adorable toddler photo—an adorable toddler who, I was pleased to admit, was me. But something else was also part of the attraction: women, then and now, look at the photo and say, "Mmm, is that a little Peter Pan collar shirt you have on there? Now, look how the straps of those little houndstooth trousers are going through the nice little loops in that Peter Pan collar shirt. Mmm, your Momma was sure dressing you." Of course, I like all that. Of course, right now, there is a whole side of me that yearns to say, "Sweetheart, I'm dressing right for being with a woman like you, and I was dressed right for being with you ever since I was three. I've been Anticipating you." With fantasies such as these, I searched for the toddler photo, and for the others, too. The hour I had to kill before my father was supposed to arrive went by as quickly as the ore boat on the Lake out the window met the horizon, then disappeared.

Another hour shot by, still no sign of my Dad. I thought about running down to the bookstore I liked on 53rd Street— the one with the fantastic fiction section that was the only one I knew of that made a point of displaying hard-to-find books from the tiniest of presses. I thought as well—and now I was starting to get pissed about being stood up—about going out and having lunch on my own. Yes, the deal had been that my father and I would meet at the apartment and then go to lunch somewhere in the neighborhood. But now I was thinking: "No deal now. I had just half a bagel and a glass of juice at break of day, and that was break of day, eastern time. I'm going out." Thinking that way gave me a rush but no momentum, no push out the door. I had never played casual with meeting my father or with any of the small measures of filial piety in all my life. And so, after I woofed and barked and stomped around the apartment, and after I even gazed longingly down from the 28th floor upon the roofs of the bookstore and a half-dozen restaurants on 53rd Street, I settled into waiting some more.

My father arrived close to 3 P.M., hidden behind an array of parcels much like a child hidden behind a cluster of balloons. I thought he had been at work but obviously he had been shopping. "Needed a few things for the trip to St. Louis tomorrow," he said, as he heaped the bags on a corner of the dining room table. The bags were from some of the choicer North Michigan Avenue men's furnishing shops. That got me to thinking about what he possibly could have needed that he didn't have (every closet brimmed with his finery), and more, what—or who—he was dressing up for in St. Louis. In his postcard, he had told me that he might have to go out of town right in the middle of my visit; that's why he suggested that I not come. I had immediately called to say that I couldn't cancel my business appointments and that we should just make the best of the couple of days we could visit together, should he really have to go out of town. Well, here it was: he was going and he was going the next day. "So, what's in St. Louis?" I asked, aware of the edge in my voice and aware, too, that we had not yet even said hello. "I'll tell you over lunch," he said, gesturing toward the door and re-buttoning his coat. And so we went out, walking stiffly together, silent with the thought that we had to get some things said.

We headed west on 53rd Street, passing under the IC tracks and arriving at the corner of 53rd and Lake Park. A glance at the Hyde Park Bank building reminded me of my business appointments in the morning; the window display at the bookstore with the great fiction section promised that I'd have at least one pleasant thing to do after my father left town.

We strolled up to a restaurant, Valois', a neighborhood institution now even more on the map because a young sociologist had just published a book, *Slim's Table*, about the middle-aged black men who gathered there for meals. Since my father had read the book and had sent me a copy of it, I thought we might be heading in there. But we weren't and one look in the window told me why: my father might have been seventy-three, but he wasn't about to resign himself to the company of frumpled old men picking at meatloaf and staring at their glasses of water. No, we were going down the street a little further to Mellow Yellow, a place brighter and younger and hipper, surprisingly so when you thought about how it was hopelessly stuck with its corny sixties' name.

We settled at a table by the window onto the street. On another day, I would have pointed out to the storefronts across the street where there were once stores like Kiddie Kicks where my sister and I would get our school shoes. But the day that lay before me and my father, or rather, what was left of it, did not seem the occasion for getting lost in simple memories. We didn't need to get lost; we needed to get on with it. "You first," I said to myself, and, as if he heard me, my father said, "Tell me again why you're here in Chicago."

It would have been grand, as they say in the novels, if I could have said, "I'm here to see you—we need to make a point of seeing each other now that Mom has died." But those phrases and the feelings behind them, while so paramount when I had planned this trip, were now lost in the pockets of a present misery. When I reached for words, what came out was, "I've been living in Connecticut for twenty years. There's no point to my still having a bank account here. I'm going to close the account in the morning. I am going to take my savings. . . ." *Home* was the last word of that sentence; I knew it and he did too.

The waiter came and took our orders. We both ordered something sensible like salads with strips of grilled chicken breast. My father tried to take advantage of this interruption and turn the subject of what I planned to do with my savings into a discussion of pension plans. "Are you still putting everything into TIAA, or do you put something in CREF?" he asked, while forking around in his salad. We'd been there before, and before, all my life it seemed, I'd given in to what seemed his plea to make a side issue the real issue until it piddled down to nothing. Ignoring his question, I fired my own: "So, what's in St. Louis?" I held him to his promise to tell me over lunch.

"I'm going to St. Louis to go to a dance," he began. "An old friend, an acquaintance of mine" (I marveled at the backtracking: "Old friend" had already become "acquaintance") "has asked me to escort her to a dance, and so I'm going." He continued, "She is the widow of a doctor we knew. When your mother and I would go to party weekends in St. Louis, they were one of the couples hosting and entertaining us. I've been seeing her for about a year. I've been meaning to tell you." He then told me her name.

I didn't respond right away and that worried him. "I've been meaning to tell you," he repeated, "but I didn't know what you'd think about my starting to see other women." He meant women other than my mother, and he sought my appreciation for his appreciation for my feelings. But this I sadly knew was another deflection, another attempt at escape from frank exchange. Aiming at straight-talk, I said, had to say, "So what you are telling me now, but couldn't tell me weeks ago, or even a week ago when you sent me that postcard, is that you are going to spend the weekend with a ladyfriend, someone you've known a long time and liked, someone you have introduced to my sister but have not even mentioned to me."

As I awaited his answer, it occurred to me that while I was trying to say, "Why haven't you talked to me, why haven't you told me this before?" what he was hearing, with ears tuned only to particular frequencies, was that even his daughter might not be able to keep something to herself. That the problem with families, he surmised, was that they were composed of family members; and that no matter whether they were mammy-made by your mother or by your wife, these family members, near and far, might write or call to ask permission to drive or fly or even walk into your life. When my sister moved from Boston to Kalamazoo, she once said to him, "I'm so close now." He said, "But I need my privacy."

And yet, once, when the woman from St. Louis was visiting, my sister visited, too. Ignoring the awkward, absurd introduction in which the ladyfriend was told of my sister that she was meeting the Supreme Court, the two women retired to a back room, genuinely made friends of each other, exchanged phone numbers, and began the then hopeful process of trying to figure out how to moderate my father's lifestyle and save him. In the months to come, when their concern offered the fragance of adoration, he was attentive, gallant. But when it took on for him the stench of intrusion, he backed away and sought the company of a new — and to us, strange — group of friends.

Right now, over a lunch I was almost too angry to eat, I was intruding, too. That, and the fact that we had never been able to go beyond opening salvos, meant that the lunch was over. (We both would have made very poor boxers for, at least with each other, we were prone to lunge and exhaust ourselves before the first bell.) "I have to get back and start packing," he said, as we both threw money on the check. The full import of that didn't dawn on me until we were actually back in the apartment and he left me alone in the living room while he retired to his bedroom and began to bustle about.

I wandered in circles, unable to settle into a chair, to distract myself with the newspaper, to pick up a book. My eye fell on the neat row of family publications, including a rather complete assembly of my own stuff, and I thought again of how artfully someone had managed to plant books and offprints in a living room without exactly displaying them. When my mother was alive, this was her classy way of expressing family pride in subtle, tailored terms. But what was being expressed now? In that room, now, each book might as well have been a lamp, a coaster.

I was peering out at the Lake, retracing the step-by-step descent of the airplane I had been on that morning, knowing that it had flown from my right to my left, a glint in the sky first above the steel mills then above the Lake then above the Loop, when my father reappeared. Something was in his hand, I soon saw it was a pair of socks. "I have to take these back," he said. "Look, they're defective." I half looked. "I'm going to take these back," he emphasized. But I never dreamt that he meant right then until I heard the jingle of his car keys. "Mother in heaven," I thought, "he's actually going down to the car and going downtown."

I should have stopped him, or at least tried to do so. But what was I going to say? Telling him he already had fifty billion pair of perfectly good socks seemed no more persuasive than pointing out I had just traveled a thousand miles to spend time with him and he ought not to go. And so he disappeared into the elevator and the garage and the teeming rush-hour traffic, determined to return his socks but really to buy another two hours of time away from me and our prickly conversation. I just waved him on, said nothing, just waved him on. It wasn't a wave of goodbye or a wave of dismissal. It was a cross between a blotting out and a benediction. I wished him well on his completely absurd journey. But also, after all the bullshit, I wanted a smoke, and with him gone that was now a possibility.

Sometime after I had furtively puffed two cigarettes while out on the balcony, too scared to enjoy them since I am deathly scared of heights, I realized that my father and I were due for dinner at the house of old, old friends in less than an hour, and he was not yet back. When it got down to twenty-five minutes before dinner, I started into one of those shake-of-your-head unbelieving laughs that you learn when your children become teenagers, and you can't believe that right when the whole family needs to go out the door to get somewhere, they suddenly want to take a shower. Right then, my father arrived, and his first words were, "I need to take my nap; missed it earlier." Why he had missed his nap and everything else that was supposed to have happened that afternoon begged to be addressed, but what I said was, "You know, we're due at the Runners in twenty minutes." "Call them," he yawned, and I did.

We were a good hour late getting to the Runners, but they were as gracious as I knew they would be and just wanted us to get in the door and be at home. Drinks were served and soon came salads, too soon, but that happens when you are late and you throw your hosts off schedule. This should have been a little party of the sort that comes naturally to people who have known each other for over forty years; I certainly was with three of the people who had raised me from birth. But there were funny awkwardnesses, lapses in conversation that were hard to fathom. I was struck by how the Runners and my Dad talked as if they hadn't seen each other in a long time, which didn't seem possible to me. Then I remembered a telephone conversation I'd had with Dorothy weeks before, when I'd called to tell her I'd be coming to town. "Of course, we're going to see you, we'll be here," she began. "But you know, you're going to have to talk to your father and check his schedule. Step's so busy. I try to get him over here. I tell him he's welcome anytime, anytime, like every Wednesday when Runner's home early. But I don't know. And I don't want to impose. . . ."

I had scoffed when I heard this. After all, Dorothy had been my mother's best friend and is my sister's godmother, and Charlie once told me that my Dad was like a brother to him. I'd thought maybe Dorothy was misinterpreting something, but here, now, as I watched my father glance at his watch or glimpse into space, I knew things were askew. Was it about my mother, was it about how the Runners and the Steptos had been young together, a foursome together, had bought a two-family building together, and lived together for years? Could it be something that sentimental yet monumentally heart-felt—or could it be something else?

My mother may have been in the glimpses into space but not in those at the watch. The watch: minutes were passing but not in the time zone of savoring memories or friendships. My father was determined not to spend his last days in the sinkhole of memories, and he was carefully measuring the time he spent with old friends. And even though he was about to fly off to St. Louis the next day, he was becoming increasingly certain that he wasn't going to spend his last days with a woman who was the friend of old friends. It smacked of prearrangement, of inevitability. Your wife dies, and your friends descend from far and near to legislate who your new mate will be. Even your children are colluding: your daughter makes friends with one of the designated desirables; your son thinks someone, even someone he doesn't know, might be good in your life.

Toward the end of dinner, I observed again how obviously my father wanted to be elsewhere, and thought about an exchange we'd had a year or two before. I was in Chicago, and we were driving to a bar in South Shore that also served Chinese food. He asked, "Do you have a bar?" "What do you mean?" "I mean," he said, "is there a place you go to meet your friends?" I had to confess I had no such bar. I thought about mentioning that at my age I was still picking up kids from school, that I still needed my evenings to prepare for classes, but I let that go. So, too, did I not comment, once we were at the bar, that the crew that crowded around him and hailed him seemed hardly friends. From the snips of conversation I heard, they struck me as sycophants and bloodsuckers, parasites eager to press on to an older man who might be able to do them some favor in the city since he had been, briefly, head of the board of health.

So, was that where Dad wanted to be? Did he want to be out at his bar? Was that why he was glancing at his watch? All I know is that as soon as dinner was over, he was out the door, saying brightly, "Going away tomorrow, have to pack." Dorothy and Charlie urged me to stay another hour, promising me a ride home. "Yes, stay," my father said. At that point, I didn't need any convincing, and I settled back into my chair.

When I got back to the apartment, later than I thought I would, my father was asleep. Whether or not he had gone to his bar, he was asleep now; the door cracked, the room dark. I lingered at the door, listening to the rise and fall of his breath, not labored but distinct in the utter quiet of the apartment. I wanted to hear him sound like he was at peace, though I doubted that he was, and yes, he sounded peaceful.

Not quite ready for bed, I went and poured myself a night-cap, then retreated back to the room I usually stay in with one of the family photo albums in tow. "This one is an old one," I said to myself as I turned the pages. "This is one from when my parents were my age." I soon came upon a photo I hadn't planned to borrow, but later did.

It's a photo of my father holding my sister, then an infant, with the blanket around her for that moment being generously open, so that the photographer can see her, but maybe too because it seems to be a warm day. My usually tall and erect father is curiously hunching down, scrunched over. My thought about this before has always been, "You can't really tell, but he's hunched like that to be closer to Jan, to have his face close to hers." But now I am wondering if his posture might also have something to do with who is next to him on his right. On my father's right is his father, as well dressed as my father is as both men are in good suits. No matter how much my father hunches and scrunches, he can't erase the fact that he is distinctly taller than his father. But maybe he wants, in this one rare moment, to minimalize the difference; maybe he wants his face closer not only to Jan's but to his father's as well. Well below the two men, Robert Louis and Robert Charles, stands a seven-year-old boy, Robert Burns. He's not in a suit like his father and grandfather, but he's dressed nicely—sport shirt, pleated slacks, a little cap on his head—his mother wouldn't have it otherwise. But he's not exactly standing. He's doing something funny with his body; it's in an odd S-curve, swerving first toward the grandfather and then at the top of the "S" toward his father and sister. The gymnastics of it all has put a contorted smile on his face, like what you see on the face of a high-jumper, whose grimace all through the process of leaping has suddenly become something else the moment he knows he's high enough in the air to make it all happen. Then you look again and note: the boy snaking his way up into the atmosphere of his menfolk, as they pose with his months-old sister, is standing on his tiptoes. That's how much I wanted to be in the picture.

In the background is brick, nothing but brick wall. It is the brickface of my grandfather's apartment building, and that alone should make it seem something other than brick, something softer. But it's brick. We in the picture are up against the wall.

Rising in the morning, I drape on my bathrobe and make my way to the front of the apartment. Immediately, I spy my father, awash in the morning light streaming in the lakefront windows, intent with the morning newspaper. Though his back is to me, I can tell he is already dressed for the day; his packed bags are near beside him, angled toward the door. "Have you already had breakfast?" I ask, moving closer. "There's cereal in the cupboard and English muffins in the fridge," he replies. "Juice and milk are in the fridge. Sorry, the milk is skim milk; that's all I use these days." From that I gather he's had breakfast.

Sensing how soon he plans to depart, I say, "Look, I don't have to be anywhere before eleven. Let me drive you to the airport. I can throw on some clothes in a minute." But as I move down the hall to dress, he replies, "Don't trouble yourself. I've called my driver. He should be here any minute." "Your driver?" I say. Having a driver was news to me. "Well," he began, "he's not my driver exclusively. Henri drives a Yellow Cab. But he has a beeper or something, and I can arrange for him to drive me without going through the dispatcher. He's very punctual and courteous. He should be here soon."

As if my father had snapped his fingers, the phone rang, and it was the doorman from the lobby announcing that Dr. Stepto's cab—Henri—had arrived. My father rose and leaned toward his bags, but I swept forward and grabbed them before he could. We went out the apartment door and down to the elevator. We must have been quite a sight: an older gentleman in a fine grey suit, striding with purpose, with a balding man behind him, disheveled in his bathrobe, struggling along with a couple of suitcases.

At the elevator we stopped and my father turned to me, handing me something. "This is Henri's card," he said. "You might like to have him take you to the airport when you go back on Sunday." I glanced down at the card in my hand. On the left appeared the logo of the Yellow Cab Company. On the right, in the same shade of yellow, was a smiley, have-a-good-day happy face. In between, was Henri's full name, "Henri Pouissant." As the elevator arrived and clunked open, it occurred to me that Henri was one of the new guys, one of the new American dreamers. Even in this detail, my father was making certain he wasn't going to be driven into the past.

From the back of the elevator, my father spoke his last words to me. "Henri drives a nice car," he said, "very clean. He's very attentive to me." Like a good son, I thought. Then the blue doors of the elevator—blue as the Lake—shut, and my father was gone. The cables behind the doors rumbled and mumbled, dropping my father down to the earth.

Vineyard

After we sold our summer house in Michigan in 1959 or so, my family had to learn some "summer behaviors" to which other folk probably had already adjusted: my father had to accommodate to having all of us around, right in Chicago, all summer; my mother had to learn to live with her mother not right around the corner—even closer in the summer than during the rest of the year; and all of us had to be schooled in the strangest activity of all: the Family Vacation Trip. The trips were strange not just because of the togetherness they enforced (no family is thrown together more than when they are traveling) but because they never were again to the Other House, and they never were exactly to the same destination. Then, too, they occurred not in the seemingly infinite sprawl between June and September, but in the small cell of time— ten days? two weeks?—that can be garishly bracketed off on a single page of a calendar.

However, certain patterns—patterns later to be seen by me as solaces—emerged from our triptaking. For one, despite the fact that Chicago is the hub of the nation and a gateway especially to everything bounding north, south, and west, our trips were invariably east; our compass knew no other direction. Another pattern, made all the more delightful because it masqueraded as a bit of whimsy, was that soon after we got to our destination—New York, for instance—someone would say, "We're so close now, why don't we go on to Martha's Vineyard?" and off we'd go.

Why we never admitted from the start that we were going to the Vineyard remains a curiosity. The answer probably lies in something as simple as our not knowing until we were East whose cottage on the island we might rent or borrow. But I liked this crazy way of going to the Vineyard; I liked the truancy, the lunacy even, of ignoring the calendar and shredding up itineraries and suddenly driving through the night to arrive at dawn on line for the ferry to the island. I yearned for these island adventures because while each transported me back to something comfortable and familiar—something like Michigan with its scrub pines, its waters and beaches, its boats and ferries, its promise of seeing old friends—each also launched me into something new and strange and magical. Coming to the island was, I see now, a ferrying into the future, a serendipitous step toward my trekking east at the age of sixteen, and then beginning to invent the life I since have had in New England.

The Vineyard we came to in the early 1960s consisted of Oak Bluffs—we really didn't know much of the rest of the island in those days. Vineyard Haven we knew because of the ferry, Gay Head we visited because of the cliffs, Chilmark existed only as a name on a map or a sign, Edgartown was where you had to go to get to South Beach, etc. Our days on the island followed simple schedules: sunny days were beach days, rainy days were spent with board games and jigsaw puzzles, evenings were full of gatherings at one house or another, but they were gatherings mostly, not parties. Of course, we traipsed out for ice cream, fudge, fried clams and everything else still vended on Circuit Avenue, but I was never in a restaurant and I don't recall my parents leaving us kids behind to go off to one. Meals were simple, casual, and often communal: hampers shared on the beach, potluck gathered on a porch, picnics spread in Waban Park. After dinner, adults would get together in each others' cottages and play cards and sometimes drink too much; teenagers would wander off to the Inkwell and sometimes leave the folksingy/doo-wop campfires and the teentalk for a ride in a car they should never had accepted. But in general, contrary to the wailings of certain Brahmin types, the island and Oak Bluffs in 1960 had hardly been ruined. The threat of that was still some thirty years away.

When I think of what threatens the Vineyard, I am reminded of a conversation I had two years ago with a cabdriver on another island, St. Thomas, in the U.S. Virgins. Granted he was a bit curmudgeonly, and determined in his way to live in another time (Billie Holiday's tunes filled his cab; No thank you! he said to reggae and rap), but what he said of how his island was endangered made striking sense. "You know what's wrong with this island now? You know what? The *problem* is that what's in New York on Monday is here by Wednesday!" Cecil (I will call him Cecil) was inveighing against the whole "urban culture" (not strictly urban, as we know, but peddled as such—recording companies now even have vice presidents for "urban music") that was hooking a whole generation into thinking that they had to be some sort of user or gangsta to be *down.* When he spied a young man stumbling down the street, stumbling one hoped only because his huge baggy pants kept falling off his behind, he said, "You know what's going on there? He's no island boy no more. He thinks he's American."

The Vineyard has island boys (and girls) desperately trying to be American; native young people in the latest hip-hop fashions practicing their walks and their slouches, feigning attitudes. But I don't think they are the young people who forced a fifty-something friend of mine (who has lived part of *all* those fifty-odd years on the island) off the Circuit Avenue sidewalk last Fourth of July, daring him to say something. Nor do I think that they were among the occupants of a sleek Continental Town Car—a car carrying drugs—that caused a fatal accident out by the airport this summer. I don't even believe that island youth are part of the new unhousebroken crowd that buys pizza slices, eats them down to the crust, and then tosses the crusts on the ground.

The perpetrators are not island youth, costumed for the street life though they often be, nor are they always youth at all. But they are Americans, or wannabe Americans of a certain stripe. They descend upon the island from America, as the mainland is increasingly called, they are—in the carefully yet clearly worded statement of the Vineyard NAACP—the "individual visitors ... so intensely focused on their own pleasures that they are less than mindful of the laws, rules, and conventions that are in place to protect everyone's right to enjoy the Island...."

That description appropriately describes the marauders who have come to the island around the Fourth of July of late, and in the words of Sterling Brown (echoing Shakespeare), they don't come by ones, they don't come by twos, they come by tens. This year's nightmare was a raucous beach party at South Beach: as if it were Myrtle Beach, not South Beach, twenty thousand "visitors" made the scene, aching to be able to say that they had partied down with the NFL and NBA superstars (what constitutes a "superstar" these days is yet another issue) who had imported themselves for the occasion. But the problems weren't confined to the beach: traffic was hopelessly snarled, stores in Oak Bluffs were "damaged" (the word the papers so fastidiously chose) in the evening hours, some house parties in Edgartown were so huge and raging that the one policeman who could be sent to the scene could not shut them down.

The meetings about what to do about this have already started. Perhaps a further indication of how America has invaded the Vineyard is that it seems impossible to discuss solutions to what the local newspapers are calling the "summer concerns" without being stymied or silenced by the potential racial implications of taking action. At a meeting—or on the beach or on a sidewalk—someone will talk of penalizing landlords for renting to rowdy tenants. But someone else will say, wait a minute, we have enough problems with landlords discriminating among tenants. Another voice sings out, arguing for buttressing the local police with state police and police dogs. In reply, someone, someone who clearly doesn't want to bring up race, speaks almost euphemistically of the "negative connotations" of troopers and dogs for "people of color." A favored solution, mentioned at one of the late summer meetings, is devising and distributing a civility card (my phrase for what it sounds like), listing ten tips for the first-time visitor to the island. I suppose this solution is getting a hearing because no one has attached a "racial implication" to it—at least not yet.

I guess I could go to the next meeting and, as a historian, point out that early in this century the Chicago Urban League had at least two civility cards that they distributed in the train stations to black migrants arriving from the South. While the cards provided information about jobs and housing, they were fundamentally about behavior: do not talk loud on streetcars; do not hang out on your porch; *do* find yourself a church, etc. So, I guess I could, in that way, go to the meeting and show that civility cards have racial implications. But I am not going to do that. If I weigh in on this civility card matter, it will not be to prevent it but to help author it. I think our ancestors at the Urban League had a good idea. The only problem will be paring down the list of tips to ten.

1991: my sister Jan calls; she has rented a house on the Vineyard, in Oak Bluffs; she invites me and my family to come for one of the weekends during her stay. Excited, I say, "Yes!" Going to the island sounds like the perfect thing to do after I finish my summer teaching up in Vermont. Then suddenly I get wary; I start asking anxious questions: "What do you do there now? Who do you see? Do you get invitations? Do you feel you have to go? Do you see anybody we knew when we were kids?" My sister starts laughing; she knows what is worrying me—she knows me.

She knows that as a youth I never joined the social clubs that were minor-league teams for the big-time fraternities awaiting in college; she knows I left Chicago at sixteen for college in Connecticut, never really to return, because I feared falling into the same dull social round for the rest of my life.

She senses, too, partly because of my odd questions about her life in Boston, that I am caught in a time warp, still back in the 1950s in my thoughts about the island—still brooding about how such a nice place could be infested with people straight out of a novel like Dorothy West's *The Wedding*.

"It's OK," she says cheerfully. "You can do what you want, *we* do what we want; you know it wouldn't be otherwise with Ricardo!" Ah yes, I think, being reminded of my Panamanian brother-in-law. He's been in Boston for nearly thirty years, he's surely figured out whether the Vineyard is negotiable, and so has my sister. Jan adds, "Perhaps you don't remember, but Ricardo and I have been coming to the island for a couple of years now. It's great, the kids love it, and you should come." Before replying, I take measure of the generosity both in her invitation and in her ignoring my foolishness. When words come to me, I say, "Yes, we're coming." Then I make our ferry reservations, still nervously expecting something, but not expecting an act of nature, a storm.

The storm comes and actually it is a full-blown hurricane. When the hurricane hits, it doesn't quite occur to me that it is a hurricane, for we in Connecticut still have power and have not lost any trees. We start driving the next day, and three hours down the road, on the Cape and near the boat to the island, I am forced to skirt around downed tree limbs in the road. Telephone and electrical cables wobble down like vines or snakes. It is becoming treacherous. The storm is over but the boding atmosphere, not just the sky, is, in Gwen Brooks's phrase, "grayed in and gray."

We reach the ferry terminal at Woods Hole, and I ask the attendant whether boats to the Vineyard are running and whether my ticket for the day before is still viable. He says,

"You can have your pick of boats." I say, "Great," it still not registering that this is scary news; that if I can drive up to Woods Hole in the middle of August and casually get on the next boat to the Vineyard, something's wrong.

Our car is one of the several joining the trucks half-filling the boat. When we debark at Vineyard Haven, we drive into more gray gloom and storm debris. A few more minutes of driving and it is clear that the hurricane has hit the Vineyard harder than the Cape, certainly much harder than it hit Rhode Island and Connecticut. Trees, not tree limbs, are down everywhere, and the gray gloom is even more intense because the island has lost power. Disconcerted by the hurricane, confused further by not remembering that an avenue on the Vineyard might be a dirt road, we nonetheless find the house my sister has rented, and we find her, and her family.

"So, you finally got here," Jan says, her arms opening to give us hugs. Chuckling, laughing about how only our family could plan a reunion the day of a hurricane, we unpack the car and make our way into the candlelit house. Soon, we are all huddled around the kitchen table, visiting, but also facing collectively how we are going to manage together a day, or days, without power. Someone goes off to count how many candles remain; another of us checks the supply of charcoal; I am sheepishly pleased with myself for remembering to bring some wine. Then we start to thinking about dinner—what can we fix, how can we cook it, who's going to do what.

It is in the midst of all this planning, this singular moment of familial provisioning and sharing, that it begins to dawn on me that I am on the island with my sister again; that we are the grownups now; that we now have spouses and children; and that we now have not just the wherewithal but the duty, strangely enough, to hear the island's call and to drive, even through the night, and the residues of storms, to the boat.

Later that evening, after most of us are abed, I sit on the porch with my sister, smelling the sea, listening to the sounds of the evening, so gentle in the wake of the hurricane. Thinking back, way back almost thirty years, I turn to her and ask, "Jan, when we were kids and came to the island, where did we stay, which house?" Even in the darkness I can see that my question has caught her by surprise. Turning to me, moving to place her hand on mine, she says, "Why, it was this house, Bobby. This house!"

Years had gone by, I'd traveled, I'd lived far afield—California, Europe—but I hadn't meant to go so far as to forget the places dear to me such as this little Vineyard house. Here was further proof of something I seemed hellbent on learning the hard way: When you take off for another life, don't be so cocksure about knowing what you are keeping and what you are losing.

When my clan gathers together these days on the Vineyard, in what is now the Other House, we are most obviously a clan of black and white Americans. More precisely, if that is possible, we are black and of New England, the Midwest, and the West, partly by way of the South, and of the West Indies, by way of Panama. We are also white and of New England and the West, partly by way of England, Ireland, Italy, and Portugal. We are also Native American, and we are probably a bunch of things we don't even know about. We came here on the Mayflower and on ships before the Mayflower; we came here on slave ships and, as the quip goes, on "every other kind of ship except the rocketship." We are a mongrel family, and in that a quintessential New World family. We show our colors when we gather, and I am especially aware of this when we gather on the Vineyard in August.

Why this is so has to do in part with ingrained habits—ingrained by the race rituals of this land—of self-observation: you look at yourself and your kinfolk on the beach or on your porch, for example, and you wonder what other people see. But it also has to do with the charged sense of race that arrives with the droves of people vacationing in August, and that is in its way another kind of late summer humidity. Indeed, in August particularly, the business of vacation has become the business of race, and that is surely the biggest change on the island since my youth.

The business of race is a story of black enterprise, whether the entrepreneurs are black or not. The products freighted in—the posters, the tee-shirts and sweats, the carvings, weavings, sculptures and curios—are not in themselves unusual, but what is striking is how they signify as race products, and how the race product has thus become a vacation memento, and a *Vineyard* vacation memento at that. There is much to observe in how some shops now have their ethnic corner or black window: one establishment might specialize in books and cards, others in apparel, others still in posters, prints, and other images. I have been scrutinizing the images lately, not to make a purchase, but rather to determine whether there are images available that do not border on the cliché. I am having little luck; maybe the good stuff is gone, maybe I'm poking around too late in the season, but I doubt it.

One poster shop I scouted, thinking that since it is new it might have an advanced marketing approach, was especially clever in its mix of island images and other images, which I will classify as country European and American urban. In this shop, and it's hardly a dumb move, urban America comes in two flavors: Seinfeld and blackfolk. My urban America, like many, is bepeopled by more than Seinfeld characters and blackfolk characters, but that is not what troubles me when I cast about this store. What troubles and grates me even is the suggestion, so rampant as I glance about, that blackfolk are only basketball players and jazz legends, or that only these images sell. Later, I walk outside and peer in the "black window," the last one around the corner from the shop's entrance. "Here we go again," I say, for here along with a print of Dizzy and a photo of Lady Day is basketball, basketball, basketball.

Some images in other businesses, notably those images with a kind of Bahian or Caribbean coloration and theme, accommodate many of the sensations I feel when I live on the Vineyard in the summer. And then there is the rush I get when I glimpse just the right, yet impossible-to-purchase, watercolor by the island's reigning black artist, Lois Mailou Jones. But we are talking market forces here, and apparently there is no real market for black images that viscerally connect with *Vineyard* life unless, of course, you take into account the proliferating images emblazoned on apparel.

I spend a shameful number of idle moments in all of my venues reading the messages on apparel, the fascinations of reading having little to do with what's new to read and much to do with two of my more raging concerns: How did this fish market (or gym or bistro or sleepy town or sportswear company, etc.) convince this bozo in front of me to buy one of their billboards and to think it cool (or whatever) to wear it? And there's this: What personal needs are being met, as the thera-

pists say—and as the scholars of autobiography say, too—
when someone goes public sporting the ethnic cap, the race
shirt, the motherland headband? "Thank God I'm Irish!"—
are you sure? "I'm Polish and You Bet I Polka!"—I want to
watch. "Free John Gotti"—whoa. "It's A Black Thing, You
Wouldn't Understand!"—don't count on it.

On the Vineyard, we're in way deep with both billboard apparel—who wouldn't want to match the paraphernalia sales
of the Black Dog Tavern and have armies of people gaily ad-
vertising for them?—and with race apparel of a certain order.
Maybe I've missed something, but even with the countless
number of Italian Americans visiting the island, and living
here, too, I've never seen anyone wearing a tee that said, "Pai-
sans on the Bluffs." No, make no mistake, aside from the
Aquinnah shirts venerating the Wampanong Indians who
were here from the beginning, race apparel on the island is
black apparel.

You can get Inkwell caps, tees, sweats, and bumperstickers,
you can find "Brothers on the Bluffs" and "Sisters on the
Bluffs" tees, though oddly not always in the same store. "It's A
Vineyard Thing" is readily available (thank God the producer
didn't print "Thing" as "Thang," but that alas would sell,
too). One garment outfit, the Masai company (I think we get
the message) has shirts with black silhouettes, hauntingly
reminiscent of the images Charles Cullen produced during
the Harlem Renaissance. In the same shop but across the way
is another black silhouette shirt, this time of a solitary black
male figure. Charles Cullen might have sketched this one, too,
though I doubt he would have captioned it, "The Black Man/
Martha's Vineyard." This shirt should be moved over closer

to the others; I don't like to see a lonesome brother shouting "The Black Man/Martha's Vineyard" when he could be
across the store fraternizing with all the bloods on the other
shirts.

Fraternity, and sorority, are indeed one of the themes in
this apparel: black Alphas and Deltas and all the rest can
readily find Vineyard garments printed up with their Greek
letters. Along these lines, but more inclusive in its group message, is the new tee announcing "It Takes an Entire Village to
Raise a Child." This is definitely one of the more clever designs, for while all the village iconography is relentlessly African (no one else lives in villages, right?), there is still a lot of
invitation here beckoning the nonblack purchaser. Who
knows? Maybe even Hillary Clinton snapped up one of these
this summer. Surely, some of her staff did.

Just as "entire village" can be read variously, as something
black or as something closer to what the face of the Vineyard
(and the nation) really looks like, the pronoun "we" is open to
interpretation as well. This is what it comes down to, I think,
as I wander the island's shopping areas: Who is the "we" on
these caps and shirts, is there room for me in that "we"—and
room for all my kinfolk, too?

There is a shirt that approximates my requirements,
though I would never buy it, and not just because I am an English teacher. It is the "We Be Jammin'/Martha's Vineyard"
tee with all the multicolored figures on it; they are the village—the we—on that shirt. It's an OK shirt, but I don't like
it, and one of the reasons I don't is that you can go down the
street and find the other version of it, the all-black figures version. Of course, this is nothing really to get het up about, this

is just the reality of doing business: somebody—maybe even one of the Masais—is smartly going after both markets, not one or the other.

But I am het up about it. For in the end, the fact that there are many "we" shirts, and some "we" shirts that can instantly be modified not just for a specific group but likely for a specific store, proves that there is little difference between the billboard shirt and the racial identity shirt, for they are all selling something. More precisely, these are shirts that ask us to *buy* into a certain notion of who we are and why we have good times on the Vineyard. The "we" of this island, and the "we" of me, must tolerate this business, but we need not fill its coffers. Why should anyone pay to wear billboards, and even make gifts of them, especially when the buying and wearing of them proves that you know no difference between espousing an identity and visiting a bakery? Did you enjoy the muffin? Buy a cap! Are you black? Buy this cap, too!

Let me confess that I do *select* the tee-shirts I bring to the Vineyard of a summer (doesn't everybody?), and that I do have one I consider my race shirt. It's a shirt from another island, St. Helena, among the South Carolina Sea Islands. It is the shirt sold by the museum at Penn Center, where one of the first schools for former slaves was founded—the school where Charlotte Forten briefly taught. There are no figures on this shirt, though the images of people the museum possesses and could have used are arresting and unforgettable. What the museum has printed on the shirt instead of human figures is a photograph of woven baskets, seagrass baskets from the island and of the sort demonstrating the heritage of St. Helena's black populations in Sierra Leone. Of course, the baskets speak of a culture and history, but Ellisonian that I am, I also sense in them an expression of possibility: provisions can fill those baskets, and the imagination can fill them, too.

I like this tee-shirt, it is my race shirt. It is an island shirt, it is a New World shirt. Its baskets, so beautifully woven, have room in them for me and mine.

I come to the island more regularly now, weekends in April, September, and October, weeks in May, June, and August. I would come in the winter and in the rawest parts of spring and fall, but our Victorian summer house with its one-inch walls and drafty windows cannot accommodate my desires to be on the island in any weather, any season. I have been here, in our house, in what I know now is the wrong season, and found myself creating errands just so I could get the car, turn on the heater, and be warm. Once, I left the island two days early just to warm up. But it is amazing, really, how uncomfortable me and mine must get before we throw in the towel and head back to Connecticut and America.

Right now, I've been on the Vineyard more than a month, having arrived in mid-August to spend a week with Jan and Ricardo and their daughter Maya (their son Miguel was in Senegal) before adventuring into the longest stay we've had on the island. The visit with them was good, a true reunion; we even had to worry our way through a terrific storm—a nor'easter that blew water in the house in seven different places—as if to commemorate our first time on the island together. The next evening, Michele and I and Jan and Ricardo went out to dinner. When drinks were served and we raised our glasses, we suddenly realized we had much to toast: Michele and I had just celebrated our thirtieth anniversary, Jan and Ricardo even more recently had celebrated their twentieth; and we were on the island again together, and we had each other.

A day later, our son Rafe arrived from New York with a friend, and two cousins, Mary Ellen and Annie, appeared from Pittsburgh. In another day, I knew that Eddie Gray, my boyhood friend from Chicago—the one who schooled me on Paul Laurence Dunbar during afternoons in Idlewild— would be arriving to his house, and that I would see his mother, Alice, too. My house was crowding, my life was filling. My seagrass baskets were brimming, too.

Now, Michele and I are alone in the house, doing something that only Grandma and Grandpa Burns did before, in Idlewild: staying up to the house beyond the family leavetakings, beyond the shop closings; staying until the trees color up and the waters chill and the hardware store is selling school supplies and roofing materials, not beach coolers. We are not staying 'til when we need to run the little heater every night, and certainly not 'til when the rains become snows. But we will be here while the island becomes the island again—beautiful, quiet, and a little homely.

So I guess that Grandma and Grandpa Burns—the grandparents I lived with for years and summered with for more years still—raised me in ways that I am still comprehending. I love boats, but I am not a boat person; I am a house person, and I get that from them. Furthermore, I am an Other House person, and I get that from them, too. Grandpa Burns worked two jobs—a laboratory job by day, a post office position by evening—at first to put three children through college. Later, he discovered that two jobs could get him a little cottage near a lake, and if they were the *right* two jobs, he could take off for his cottage in June and not come back to the city until Labor Day. Then he retired, and found even more weeks for himself by the lake and in the woods.

I think Grandpa Burns wanted to die up there in Michigan. Grandma went along with Grandpa winterizing the cottage, step-by-step, and installing a modern furnace, too—it kept him busy. But there was no way that she was going to isolate herself, away from her church and her friends. She won out, of course, and their last days were infinitely more comfortable for them in Chicago than they would have been in Idlewild. And they were more comfortable for us as well: my sister Jan, for example, got the chance to live with Grandma and Grandpa, after they moved in with us, just as I had lived with them twenty years before. Jan and I talk about this, sometimes while visiting on the Vineyard. We both say this is something we share, and that our lives are what they are because, as Jan put it one evening, "Well, you know Grandma and I *talked*!" I talked with her, too, and I remember how in those conversations she played with all the nicknames for Robert. She called me her Robin, she christened me her Bobolink.

The grand retirement to Idlewild, to the Other House, did not occur. But I still must give my grandpa a thousand gold stars for dreaming, for fantasizing that a simpler way of life might be just what he needed after forty years in Chicago, during which he'd seen the street outside his house turn from something barely paved into a multi-laned outlet for an expressway. No, any sane man knew that he needed to find some county roads and country roads where driving thirty or forty miles a hour wasn't endangering but rather pleasuring and good common sense. Grandpa would have liked the Vineyard bumper sticker that reads, "Slow Down! You're Not Off-

Island Anymore!" though he was a far gentler man than the irascible types who are fondest of sporting that sticker. He also would have approved of my walking to the post office for my mail, and of the times when I join in the banter about the place. His sole suggestion would have been, "But can't you find some woods to walk through along the way? The mail is better, and so are those groceries you need, after a walk in the woods."

Grandma and Grandpa were woodswalkers, deerstalkers, though they did not seek deer to kill them. Their preoccupations with deer were those of naturalists: they wanted to record species, observe does with their young, count the points on antlers, then retreat home for strong coffee, sweetened with canned milk, and buttered bisquits. Even later, when age set in and their bones stiffened and they had to drive more than half the way in their ancient Oldsmobile to their favorite sighting grounds, they roused themselves and went: nothing better made for a good morning in Michigan. After a morning like that, after communing with the woods and with each other, you were ready for the chores and the rest of the day. This was what they were remembering when they named their Idlewild cottage "Deerpath;" this in part was what Grandma Burns was recalling in her last days, years after Ocie had passed, when she spoke of the ease of their living together. This is the ease I seek in my own marriage, and which seems closest at hand when we till our land, hike a path, walk the island.

Recently, I discovered in a 1910 census record that Grandma Burns was born in 1884 in Indian Territory, in what would later become Oklahoma. This suggested strongly that Grandma was a year older than she always said she was, and

BLUE AS THE LAKE

when I reported this to Jan, she said, "Didn't I tell you that I heard some of the church ladies say at Grandma's ninetieth birthday party that the party was a year late?" We both giggled at that. But the business about being born in Indian Territory drew no chuckles; if true, if Grandma had been born there and not in Plattsburg, Missouri, as reported before, then we knew that I had stumbled across new information that maybe even our mother, Grandma's daughter, hadn't known. More to the point, it got me to thinking that Grandma had a history that commingled with that of one or another of the "Five Civilized Tribes"—the Cherokee, the Choctaw, the Creek, the Chickasaw, the Seminoles—that were removed to Indian Territory. Perhaps in this way, too, though clearly not in a way spoken of, she shared affinities with Grandpa, sensibilities that were part of the flow of undercurrents directing their relationship and how they spent their time.

Grandpa wasn't born in Indian Territory (though anything seems possible now, after finding that record for Grandma). He was born on a farm in Missouri's Buchanan County, up near where Missouri and Iowa and Kansas all converge. On his father's side at least, Grandpa's racial heritage was mysterious: certainly black and white (he had a white grandfather) but probably Native American as well. Grandpa looked Indian, and then there was his name, Ocie, arguably the most popular diminutive for Osceola, the great Seminole chief who was indisputably Indian and black. Black people in the 1880s, who had been born just before the Civil War as Ocie's parents had, knew something firsthand about the travails afflicting blacks and Indians alike; they did not idly name a child after Osceola.

Back when I was a boy, Grandpa was Grandpa; I never thought about his race, or mix of races, or about the deeper implications of his name. But when I consider these things now, and see him in my mind's eye bursting out of the Michigan woods, his copper skin aglow against the greenness of the trees and the paleness of the sandy path, I think I see a black man turning back the clock and living into all of his names, all of his races, not one. Who wouldn't want to retire *there?* I tell myself, realizing finally that "there" is not merely a spot of geography. "There" is a wholeness, a peace.

The Vineyard is my Idlewild, or rather, I am in the process of seeking on the Vineyard the sense of well-being I believe Grandpa Burns found in Idlewild. Already, I have a good start, for the Vineyard is the place where I see my sister and her family and childhood friends like Ed Gray as well as college friends and still newer friends, including islanders. The Vineyard is a place where my wife Michele is at ease in part because when she is there she is as close as she has ever lived to the settlements of her ancestors across Vineyard Sound. It is a place where our sons have found work and occasional serenity; it is the place where the children of my Pittsburgh clan come see us and give us joy before heading off to another college year. All this is key, essential, and yet above all for me, the Vineyard is where my boyhood and adulthood collide and converge. It is where my inherited woodland, freshwater Midwest self and my invented shoreline, saltwater New England self look at each other—and embrace.

A few weeks ago, I set out walking on the island near our house and near the bluffs above Nantucket Sound. A car approached and I soon saw that the driver was an old friend. As he got closer, he leaned out and waved, saying, "Welcome home!" Terribly pleased, I grinned and waved back. What a nice greeting, I thought, but then I considered how welcoming me home to the Island is still, in a real sense, premature. I have a house I come to here, but I am still in the process of being at home here. But that will come, that will come.

Credits and Sources

Three of these essays appeared previously in *Callaloo:* "Idlewild" in *Callaloo* 14:1 (1991); "Black Piano" in *Callaloo* 19:1 (1996); and "Hyde Park" in *Callaloo* 20:1 (1997). "Idlewild" also appears in Robert Pack and Jay Parini, eds., *American Identities: Contemporary Multicultural Voices* (Hanover: University Press of New England, 1994). Two other essays published before are "Washington Park" in Genevieve Fabre and Robert O'Meally, eds., *History and Memory in African-American Culture* (New York: Oxford University Press, 1994), and "Woodlawn" in *New England Review* 17:1 (1995).

Personal memories and family stories are at the heart of each essay, but most of the essays would not have the heft I believe they have if I had not supplemented the memories and stories with library research. Here are the principal sources I consulted.

IDLEWILD: Helen C. Chesnutt, *Charles Waddell Chesnutt: Pioneer of the Color Line* (Chapel Hill: University of North Carolina Press, 1952); Benjamin C. Wilson, "Idlewild, Michigan, 1912–1930: Growth of One of America's Oldest Black Resorts," *Journal of Regional Cultures* (1982), 57–70; Benjamin C.

Wilson, *The Rural Black Heritage Between Chicago and Detroit, 1850–1929* (Kalamazoo: New Issues Press, Western Michigan University, 1985).

WASHINGTON PARK: St. Clair Drake and Horace Cayton, *Black Metropolis: A Study of Negro Life in a Northern City* (New York: Harcourt, 1945); Lorraine Hansberry, *To Be Young, Gifted, and Black* (New York: Signet, 1970); Robert L. Reid and Larry A. Viskochil, eds., *Chicago and Downstate* (Chicago and Urbana: University of Illinois Press, 1989).

WOODLAWN: James R. Grossman, *Land of Hope: Chicago, Black Southerners and the Great Migration* (Chicago: University of Chicago Press, 1989); Nicholas Lemann, *The Promised Land: The Great Black Migration and How It Changed America* (New York: Knopf, 1991); Mary Mebane, *Mary* (New York: Viking, 1981).

UP TO BALTIMORE: John L. Clark, "The 351st Field Artillery History, A. E. F. 1918," *351st Field Artillery Reunion Booklet*, August 1942, pp. 11–26—I thank my Pittsburgh cousin Carl Kohlman for procuring a copy of this for me from the Carnegie Library; William O. Ross and Duke L. Slaughter, *With the 351st in France* (Baltimore: Afro-American, 1923); Emmett J. Scott, *The American Negro in the World War* (Chicago: Homewood, 1919; rpt. as *Scott's Official History of the American Negro in the World War* (New York: Arno, 1969); Robert L. Stepto(e)'s dispatches of September 22 and November 24, 1918, from France to the Pittsburgh *Courier*—I thank Eleanora Stepto Toliver for copies.

MISSOURI WEATHER: John Chilton, *The Song of the Hawk: The Life and Recordings of Coleman Hawkins* (London and New York: Quartet Books, 1990); Marcia Greenlee, "Interview with Inabel Burns Lindsay, May 20–June 7, 1977," in Ruth Edmonds Hill, ed., *Black Women Oral History Project* (Westport, CT: Meckler, 1990), vol. 7; E. L. McDonald and W. J. King, *History of Buchanan County and St. Joseph, Mo.* (St. Joseph: Midland, 1915); LaMoyne Mason Matthews, *Portrait of a Dean: A Biography of Inabel Burns Lindsay,*

Credits and Sources

First Dean of the Howard University School of Social Work, Ph.D. dissertation, Howard University, 1976.

LESTER LEAPS IN: I could invent Lester (briefly Marge's husband before Rog) after reading William Howland Kenney, *Chicago Jazz: A Cultural History, 1904–1930* (New York: Oxford University Press, 1993).

BLACK PIANO: Richard Wright's *Native Son* (1940) provides a portrait of the neighborhood in which my mother taught school.

HYDE PARK: Mitchell Duneier is the young sociologist who wrote *Slim's Table: Race, Respectability, and Masculinity* (Chicago: University of Chicago Press, 1992).

VINEYARD: I was reading various issues of the Vineyard *Gazette* and the Martha's Vineyard *Times,* Summer and Fall, 1997. The Vineyard NAACP statement appeared in the *Times,* September 11, 1997.

Acknowledgments

With gratitude, I acknowledge the support of many colleagues: Richard Brodhead, Hazel Carby, the late Michael Cooke, Ezra Griffith, Dolores Hayden, David Levin, Andrea Lunsford, Eric McHenry, Jim and Lucy Maddox, Robert O'Meally, Carlo Rotella, Charles Rowell, Jacqueline Jones Royster, and Laura Wexler. Michael Harper and David Huddle deserve special mention: they read every page and drew on their considerable skills as writers to offer the best sort of advice. Deb Chasman, my editor at Beacon, has been quite simply the perfect editor.

This is in one guise a "family book," and I thank my family for reminding me of, or leading me toward, our own hoard of family stories, facts, and lies. I turned often to Carl Kohlman, Jan Stepto Millett, Gabriel Burns Stepto, Herman Stepto, Melanie Grace Stepto, Charles Thornton, and Eleanora Stepto Toliver. Needless to say, before they died a few short years ago, my parents, Anna Burns Stepto and Robert Charles Stepto, were people I also turned to for family lore and much, much else. In this family category, I also include Dorothy and Charles Runner, Susan Runner Gold, Shari Runner Carnegie, Edward Gray, and Michael Harper.

Books get propelled along when authors have special readers, readers who are in some sense muses. My special readers were Rafael Hawkins Stepto and Michele Stepto.